RINGING THE CHANGES

Ringing the Changes is a realistic and practical guide that provides ideas, information and advice for women planning a return to work or study after a career break. Gill Dyer, Gina Mitchell and Moira Monteith draw widely upon their experiences both as tutors and as women juggling with the conflicting demands of personal and work commitments.

This invaluable book contains case studies illustrating the problems faced by women returners, and exercises designed to develop communication skills and build self-confidence. The text is accompanied by Angela Martin's humorous and delightful cartoons.

Ringing the Changes is essential reading for both tutors involved with women returners and for women contemplating the return to work or study.

Gill Dyer is a writer and editor in the Department of Employment, specializing in training matters. She has taught in further and higher education and has recently been on secondment to the BBC developing a training service for BBC SELECT.

Gina Mitchell left school at fifteen and did a variety of low-paid and unskilled jobs before going to university as a mature student with two children. She is now head of the Access Unit at the Centre for Continuing Education, University of Bradford.

Moira Monteith was the first member of her family to go to university and found the experience rather intimidating at first. She organized, together with Gill Dyer, the New Opportunities for Women courses at Sheffield Polytechnic. She is currently Head of the Centre for Information Technology and Business Education at Sheffield Polytechnic.

RINGING THE CHANGES

A woman's guide to self-development
and returning to work

*Gill Dyer, Gina Mitchell,
and Moira Monteith*

London and New York

First published 1991
by Routledge
11 New Fetter Lane, London EC4P 4EE

Simultaneously published in the USA and Canada
by Routledge
a division of Routledge, Chapman and Hall Inc.
29 West 35th Street, New York, NY 10001

Set in 10/12 pt Bembo by Intype, London
Printed and bound in Great Britain by Clays Ltd, St Ives plc.

British Library Cataloguing in Publication Data
Dyer, Gill
Ringing the changes.
1. Women. Employment
I. Title II. Mitchell, Gina III. Monteith, Moira
650.14082

Library of Congress Cataloging-in-Publication Data
Dyer, Gillian.
Ringing the changes: a woman's guide to self-development and
returning to work / Gill Dyer, Gina Mitchell, Moira Monteith:
illustrated by Angela Martin.
p. cm.
Includes bibliographical references and index.
1. Vocational guidance for women—Great Britain. 2. Career
changes—Great Britain. 3. Career development—Great
Britain. 4. Women—Education—Great
Britain. 5. Continuing education—Great
Britain. 6. Women—Employment re-entry—Great Britain.
I. Mitchell, Gina II. Monteith, Moira III. Title.
HF5382.67.G7D94 1992
650.14′082—dc20   91–10358

ISBN 0–415–05549–0

CONTENTS

ACKNOWLEDGEMENTS

We would like to thank the following authors for permission to quote from their work:

Linda Brooke "Food and the Environment", unpublished essay; Jacqueline Brown, the poem 'o' from her collection of poetry published by The Littlewood Press, The Nanholme Centre, Shaw Wood Road, Todmorden OL14 6DA; Ivana Cooke *Women Mean Business* (Everywoman 1990); Anne Dickson *A Woman in Your Own Right* (Quartet 1982); Arthur Eperon *Encoré – Traveller's France* (Pan 1983); Liz Hodgkinson *Working Woman's Guide* (Thorsons 1985); and Laura Mitchell *Simple Relaxation* (John Murray 1985).

We would also like to express our grateful thanks to all the women who have helped with their advice and support and, in particular, those who have written pieces for us to include, either as case studies or other items: Iffat Ansari, Georgina Bower, Gill Cheaney, Suzanne Dean, Enid, Jacky Fisher, Marilyn Hale, Brenda Hoskyns, Kathryn James, Janet, Kathleen Jarman, Bernice O'Mara, Valerie Radford, Devi Sorefan, Felicity Skelton, Jackie Smith, Esmé Talbot, and Judith Walker.

INTRODUCTION

Over the past twenty or more years there have been many developments and some improvements in women's social and economic situation. Even if a woman's prime responsibility is to the home and family, this does not mean domestic servility or even drudgery as it might have done one hundred years ago. Few people would seriously challenge women's right to equal pay for equal work, equal opportunities, equal political representation, pension rights and so on. However, sticking-points can be crèches, maternity leave and, more basically, sharing out domestic chores in the home, all of which would help women economically and socially. Many women feel that there is still a long way to go before women are regarded as equal to men. Nevertheless, women in all walks of life, of all ages, are challenging accepted conventions, widening their horizons and looking for new opportunities. This book is for them.

The 1990s are witnessing increased interest in women's opportunities both from women themselves and from society generally. *Ringing the Changes* takes a realistic look at the prospects and possibilities ahead.

It is a book of ideas and suggestions for women who are seeking, adapting to or just coping with change. It is especially for women who want to return to paid employment after a domestic gap, who would like to return to learning or who are considering retraining for a different kind of job. It is a guidebook rather than a blueprint. It is not a standard recipe of ingredients to change your life magically and effortlessly. There is no easy formula that will make you into a superwoman. Instead we hope that there is something here that is realistic and helpful to your situation now or in the future. Think of it like a map. You

1

wouldn't embark on a long journey in unknown territory without one. Or learning to swim: if you were shipwrecked, it would be better to know how to swim than just to drift with the tide and land up anywhere but where you want to be. Although women often share common experiences and problems and can offer support to and learn from each other, the way *you* take yourself forward is up to you.

It is not necessary to work through the book from the first to the last chapter in that order – some sections will be more relevant to you than others and you may well want to concentrate on those that interest you most. However, you may find that, having read the chapter on, say, finding a job, you wish to go back to the one on self-assessment or organizing your private life because they then become more relevant. Or you may already have a job but feel in a rut and want to make some more basic changes to your life. In which case the job-hunting chapter may not be for you but other chapters will be.

It is worth pointing out that the process of returning to work or to study may take a while. Even at a time when 'women returners' are much sought after by employers because of a drop in the number of young people leaving school and going out to work, bear in mind that finding the right job, the right course or even the right life-style may mean a longish wait. Be patient and above all be realistic. It probably helps to have a sense of humour as well.

Some people will have quite specific needs and aspirations or a well-established career to return to. Others will not know what they want to do and may have a fair bit of exploring, even self-discovery, to do. It is more realistic to take one step at a time – decisions that you take today may not bear fruit for three, four or five years to come. For instance, if you want to be an accountant or become a nurse, there will be several years of study ahead but you can start the ball rolling by joining an access or basic training course which will put you on the first rung of the ladder.

Case study

Gill Cheaney was a secretary before she married and then spent many years abroad because her husband worked for an international telecommunications company. However, within three weeks of arriving in a new country she had found herself a job. 'I'm not a coffee-morning sort of person, so I decided I'd find the best job I could in the circumstances to keep my hand in.' Since settling back in England, Gill has worked for a number of firms and is now a senior project manager at the Stock Exchange. The jobs she had abroad all helped when it came to looking for work back home although it was several years before her strategy paid off.

Ringing the Changes can be read alone or you may prefer to read it at the same time as friends and discuss it as you go along. You might want to work through it with a group of friends that already meets regularly, such as a mother-and-toddler group. Working through the material in this book as a group can be a valuable experience. It will mean you can share ideas and experiences, do the exercises together as a group and get feedback and support from each other. The book also makes a good basis for an access or women returners' course and so it will be useful to adult education tutors and facilitators.

To get the most out of *Ringing the Changes* you will need to be clear about your personal objectives and what you intend to gain. The first chapter gets you to think about where you are now and where you want to go. Thinking about and laying the foundations for a return to work or any other big change in your life, such as retirement, is time well spent and will mean a greater chance of success later on. You may be lucky – the right job or training course might drop into your lap but it is doubtful. Life just isn't like that. The most successful people are those who create their own luck.

From time to time we all probably need to sit down and take stock, to think clearly about where we are going, about our past experiences and what we have learnt from them, about our strengths and weaknesses, and about what we need to do to prepare for any eventual transition in life. It's probably time that most of the readers of this book sat down and took stock of their skills, talents and experience and began to think in terms of their usefulness to, for example, an employer. Even if a good deal of time has been spent at home with small children or elderly relatives, very few of us actually start from scratch when we are seeking a job.

If you have been at home for a period of time, it's easy to lose touch and lose confidence. But women tend to underestimate their capabilities so it is important not to be too modest about skills and talents even if you haven't been paid for them recently. A mature woman has a lot to offer an employer, especially maturity.

The message of Chapter One is to be ready for the moment when you do get your 'lucky break'. Don't expect it to come without some effort on your part. Many people, unfortunately a lot of them women, wait around passively for life to happen to them. They make excuses for themselves, looking around with envy and resignation at other people's successes. As women we tend to hold ourselves back. Many of us were taught to take a passive, low-risk view of life. We were encouraged either not to develop specific plans or to keep our plans flexible in order to accommodate our (future) husbands and families and their needs. Setting goals for ourselves goes against our training. We hope that Chapter One, 'Getting to Know You', will help you set your life goals even if it doesn't lead to the most glamorous, well-paid job on earth.

One change inevitably means changes elsewhere and involves the need to adapt and make arrangements, even compromises. Research shows that the majority of women do most of the chores at home even when they work full-time outside the home as well. Women have to be good organizers and juggle several responsibilities at the same time. The line between public and private life, job and home, is less rigid for women than it is for men. So we suggest you spend rather more time considering how your life is organized *as a whole* and discuss this with partners, friends and family.

Chapter Two, 'Women Take Credit: Organization of Private Life', picks up themes mentioned elsewhere in the book (for example, how you can manage your time), and it considers this in relation to other responsibilities, your goals for the next few years and your own needs for relaxation and recreation. We suggest you work positively at co-operation (a feature of much female activity) and at developing contacts, or even realizing how many you have already. You will need to increase the amount of control you have over your life. So you must be prepared to make definite decisions about money and, if necessary, child care. Chapter Two also considers the possibility of stress and what you might do about this.

The relationship between women and language is examined in

a practical way in Chapter Three, 'Speaking and Writing: Women and Language'. We all admire people who can speak and write fluently and most of us need to improve these skills in one or two respects at least. That is why we have included a chapter on speaking and writing. Improving communication skills can lead to greater self-confidence and often better interaction on a day-to-day basis. It may also lead to a different direction in terms of jobs as you become more assured, more prepared to offer your opinions and take on posts that require more decisive speaking. If you want to read more about language there are some recommended titles in the Reading List.

The chapter on language is divided into a range of exercises. It is concerned with helping individuals to improve their speaking skills and develop their writing capacities. It deals with speaking in small groups and large meetings, and also considers the nature of mixed-sex conversations. Finally, we consider how women can employ their knowledge of language-use to good effect.

The writing exercises deal with both public and private aspects, and also the central act of compiling a work autobiography and devising an ideal job advertisement and job specification. These last exercises build upon the work done on self-evaluation in Chapter One.

Getting back to paid employment may be the main reason for reading this book. Chapter Four, 'Finding Work', covers most of the issues and problems you will need to know when looking for work. It looks at what is involved in job-hunting and what you might be up against, and points you in the direction of sources of help and information. If you are not used to it, the prospect of having to undertake a successful job search and 'selling' yourself can be a bit daunting – particularly if you haven't done it for some years or are thrust into the position with little warning and inadequate preparation.

If you feel a bit rusty or are lacking in self-confidence, take heart, this chapter will help you brush up on job-hunting skills. A successful job search needs to be well organized. You may need to do some market research before you identify a possible plan of action. If you are having no luck you may need to review how you are going about things and possibly change direction.

'Finding Work' looks at various work options such as flexihours, part-time work, job-sharing, free-lancing, self-employment or starting a co-operative venture. It also considers the employment picture in its broadest sense. There is advice on making job applications and on the all important interview techniques. The chapter concludes with a brief mention of rights at work once you've got there.

Chapter Five, 'Learning How to Learn', will provide you with the means to deal successfully with the demands of a wide range of courses, be they educational or training. It is worth reminding yourself that the expertise developed on these courses is often invaluable when transferred to the world of work, where the abilities of communicating clearly, knowing how to separate trivia from important issues and operating in a systematic and well-organized manner are seen as essential and much sought-after skills.

If you haven't studied anything in the formal sense for a long time you will probably need to start at the beginning and follow all the steps through to the end. But, if you already know where you need to improve your performance, you can be selective in how you use the material.

As you read Chapter Five, you may become aware of the existence of new methods of teaching and learning. In the past there was often great reliance upon textbooks and formal class teaching. Now there is a growing emphasis upon the need to understand the process of learning itself and how this comes about through the application of different skills and abilities. You will certainly need to be able to read books and other written material efficiently, but you may also be required to use video or film on a course. Examinations still exist but work that is done during a course is increasingly taken into consideration. Perhaps most important of all is the new focus on the importance of personal as well as intellectual development which is emerging more and more in education and training.

Practical help and guidance which are relevant to all these issues can be found in this chapter. Study techniques are explained in detail. You can try them out on your own or with friends, using practical exercises, model answers and checklists against which to measure progress and identify strengths and weaknesses.

Tutors could use the material in a variety of ways. For example, it could provide a core study skills programme around which a course or project could be organized to meet the needs of a given group. Alternatively units can be extracted to cater for individual study problems. This approach is especially useful because it allows everyone concerned to work at her own pace.

The final chapter, 'Looking to the Future', examines changing employment patterns and realistically assesses job prospects for women in the light of developments in work, leisure, technology and so on. Various institutions and organizations which help women at work in a general sense are also mentioned. Without wishing to be over-optimistic, it is fair to say that the decade ahead may offer many opportunities and advantages for women; at least it will be a watershed in women's rights and opportunities. Changes in demographic patterns and new technology may benefit women. Discrimination and sexism will not end overnight but attitudes are changing. Many companies are offering career break schemes or part-time options and some are running special training courses to help women gain a foothold, and women themselves are becoming more confident and assertive.

Women in the 1990s are in a better position to take advantage of these changes than their mothers or grandmothers before them. After the Second World War ended, women who had helped the war effort by working in factories and offices had to return to the home to make way for the returning men. People are more aware of this 'injustice' now, and we can be hopeful that it would not happen again in the twenty-first century.

It is hoped that *Ringing the Changes* will contribute to creating a situation where equality of opportunity is *really* equal.

1

GETTING TO KNOW YOU

In order to get the most out of *Ringing the Changes* you will need to be clear about what you hope to gain. This chapter will help you to think about your goals in life in a positive and constructive way in the light of changes you may be seeking or are already having to cope with.

- If you are thinking of a return to work after some years of life at the 'sink-face',
- if you are vaguely dissatisfied with things as they are or feel in a rut,
- if you need to polish or update old skills or feel you missed out on training or education when you were younger,
- if you think that you have let opportunities slip by . . .

this chapter may set you on the road towards more fulfilling or rewarding work, offer you encouragement and help you take control of your life. Talking like this about positive and constructive change may sound a little glib, especially if the changes are unwelcome, or if you think you've missed the boat, or don't know what you want to do and think you're too old anyway! Facing and dealing with change is never simple whether you are young or old, male or female. Women have the added disadvantage of, generally speaking, being undervalued by society or undervaluing themselves and lacking confidence.

Thousands of women have faced the problems associated with returning to work or creating a new life for themselves. It's not easy but then, as someone once said, the important things in life are rarely easy and the easy things are rarely important. Don't expect miracles, even after reading this chapter.

Despite this note of caution and even if becoming a more sorted-

out and self-confident person doesn't seem a number one priority,
reading this particular chapter may provide food for thought.
Taking more control over your life and your career in a planned
way is no bad thing and can be done whether you consider
yourself to be old or young, whether you are in paid employment
or not. Life bounds along at a fairly rapid pace so we don't
usually take stock of our lives, our likes and dislikes, our strengths
and weaknesses or where we are heading. Added to this, women
who are at home looking after young children or other dependants or servicing busy husbands rarely have time to think about
their own needs or interests. Thinking of our own needs or trying
to get control is not something that comes naturally to us as
women. We tend to let others take the initiative and make
decisions on our behalf. We hold ourselves back, we fear independence and we don't take risks. We tend to make excuses for
ourselves, we wait for 'Prince Charming' to come along rather
than going out and looking for 'him' and we don't take our
careers seriously; we tend to anticipate failure. That is what we

9

are 'trained' to do; it comes 'naturally' to us to be self-effacing, unassertive and dependent.

Taking a look at yourself and setting goals is a good place to start and one of the most valuable things you can do for yourself. If you know where you are going, then you are more likely to get there. However, it is not necessarily easy or straightforward and it requires a considerable degree of effort and honesty to discover what it is you really want for yourself. We hope the effort will help the process of getting back to work or study, increase your sense of worth and give you greater insight into other people as well as yourself.

Look at yourself

Women spend most of their lives looking after the needs of others and many experience strong feelings if they decide to look after themselves for a change. They may feel self-indulgent and consequently guilty. Feelings like this may occur because examining our own lives may remind us of all the plans we haven't made and all the aspirations we haven't yet realized. We may feel sad or frightened when thinking about life goals. It is important to remember that it is not the goals which are causing these feelings. These feelings were there before and may have been a block on achieving what we want. Once you have a clearer picture of what you want in life, your subconscious and conscious mind can work together to achieve it. You owe yourself the space and time to think and work through some of these 'looking at self' exercises.

Most people find them helpful and revealing once they get accustomed to the idea. You may find it helpful to work through some of the exercises suggested here with a group of friends. a group can provide support and feedback and make you realize that you are not alone, that there are a lot of you with the same feelings of apprehension and even inadequacy. You may feel awkward at first, so group sessions used to discuss or reveal yourself and others should be handled sensitively.

'I am . . .'

One relatively straightforward, informal kind of self-assessment exercise is to complete ten 'I am . . .' sentences: for example, 'I am intelligent', 'I am happy'. Another is to write down five

10

positive and five negative things about yourself: 'I am reliable' and so on; 'I am boring'; 'I am disorganized' or whatever. If you do this in a group, participants should form pairs and discuss the sentences with each other. General discussion of the completed sentences can cover how we identify ourselves, whether we undervalue ourselves and whether we are positive or negative. You might also like to add to this a list of 'I would like to be' descriptions.

Examining what kind of person you are can help your self-development and can also help you to recognize that you might be more suited to some kinds of work or some work environments than to others. If you are methodical and independent, you might be suited to self-employment; if you are outgoing and sociable, you may find working alone difficult. Work can be stressful when it requires qualities you just don't possess. With this in mind why not try making a list of your personality traits? For example, sociable, active, assertive, etc. You don't have to take a long time over this list; do it reasonably quickly – it's not an intelligence test! Forget those characteristics you are not sure about and come back to them later. You could highlight the areas you think you need to work on. Using everyday examples, think about the qualities you have picked out. How have these traits demonstrated themselves recently or in the past and how do you think they can help you in the future? Despite the fact that it is difficult to recognize and come to terms with our failings, put some effort into thinking about them. We all have weak points; if you can't or don't want to change them, at least recognize that you have some so that you don't land yourself in a situation where they would be inappropriate.

Another way of getting a fuller picture of yourself would be to ask a friend or partner to look at your list and ask them to tick those they think best describe you. You may get a shock – a pleasant one, we hope. You might think you are nervous and indecisive and they see you as assertive and well organized. Of course, we can't be all things to all people and people will see you differently depending on the context in which they usually meet you. You could ask your friends what kind of job they see you doing.

There are quite a few exercises of a similar kind. On New Opportunities for Women, Wider Opportunities for Women or Fresh Start courses, the tutor may do what is called a 'life collage' with a group of students. This involves making a collage out of pictures and text cut out from magazines. The group would be provided with a supply of women's magazines, large poster-size pieces of paper and some scissors, glue and felt pens. The idea is to cut out anything that illustrates self-image at three stages in life: (i) up to starting work; (ii) from then until the present; and (iii) the future. Participants then stick them on the large sheet of paper in three zones representing the three stages. Written comments can be added. The completed collage is not meant to be a scientifically accurate portrait but it will register in a non-verbal way the major life themes, roughly the kind of person you think you were, are and would like to be. Students are encouraged to be as imaginative as they like – for instance a picture of a flower or a caged bird can say more than more literal material.

This exercise is used in courses because it can be fun to do even if people are not good at art or craft-type activities. It serves as an 'ice-breaker' – it gets everyone going and helps them relax and get to know other members of a group. After making the collage, the tutor or facilitator might ask people to consider why certain sections of a completed collage are overcrowded or empty, why it is, or is not colourful or if there are any threads running through the three sections – significant symbols, images and so on.

Lifeline

Another exercise which helps you take a strategic view of your past, present and future is known as 'lifeline'. Looking at past events and thinking about them helps to construct a framework which can then be used to plan future events. It may help to uncover a pattern or a cycle of repeated mistakes, which can then be avoided.

Take a large sheet of paper and draw a line across the page like this:

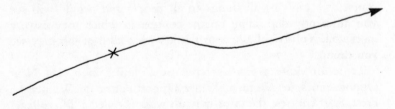

This line represents your life; one end is the beginning, your birth, and the other will represent the end. Mark a cross at some point along the line to signify where you are now. Between the beginning and this point, mark a cross for all the important events in your life and briefly describe in words or images their significance. Start as far back as possible with your first memory.

Another way of doing this is to draw a line vertically down the centre of the page (see Figure 1), the top being when you were born, and the bottom, you today. Down the line you can mark significant events (you can write these out or draw pictures) and your major achievements in life, including examination passes, prizes and jobs gained or done successfully. You will probably find one memory leads to another and that you have done more than you think, and all this adds to your experience. On the right-hand side of the line, draw or write in the things you have gained or learned from each event you have marked. On the left-hand side record the down side of these events – any difficulties or problems encountered. There may have been times of unhappiness or frustration, fear and a sense of failure.

When you have done this you might want to list those events that have changed your life and whether they came about because of your making a decision or someone else doing it for you. You could ask yourself what effects the negative things have had – have they prevented you doing something in your life? Would you have done anything differently?

You could redraw your lifeline in terms of its ups and downs. If you think you made or are making progress, your line should be pointing upwards; a horizontal line means no change and drawbacks or disasters will mean your line will go downwards.

The whole process should enable you to be more objective about yourself and to have a clearer picture of your achievements and what you plan to do next.

Who are you?

Yet another way to help you take stock is to look at your roles in life. Think about the many roles and responsibilities you have. For instance you may be 'mother', 'sister', 'neighbour' and 'customer' all in one morning. Normally with roles, there is a set of accepted rules to play by and sometimes our roles are not chosen but thrust upon us. Do you behave in the same way when you

LIFELINE EXERCISE

Negative	Born 1958	Positive
Didn't like arithmetic. Didn't feel clever enough	Started School	Liked art and craft made lots of friends
very competitive School, didn't like system. Felt a failure	Secondary School	Did lots of sport; chosen for school teams. B stream 3 CSEs 1 O level
Rows at home about make-up, boyfriends etc.	Secretarial Course	Did well on course and developed more social life and independence.
	Left home, first job	
Found I didn't really like secretarial work.	Changed jobs	Liked challenge of new job and given a lot more responsibility
A lot more work, running a flat, cooking and working	got married	Happy about new era in my life In love!!
	Moved to new area	
Felt a bit like a fish out of water	worked for insurance company	Helpful and understanding boss. Encouraged me to take insurance exams
Felt isolated and tired a lot of the time	First Child born	Felt justified, discovered new interests in the home and neighbourhood
Wanted a way of getting back to work and earning money	Took art courses and worked in voluntary organization	Found could combine motherhood and work outside home

Figure 1 Lifeline exercise

14

are 'mother' as when you are 'daughter', or when you are 'wife' and 'friend'? What would happen if you behaved differently – who would notice most and complain? Which role is 'you'? Number the roles in order of importance to you. Which role would mean the most to you in terms of loss or readjustment if you were to lose it?

Confidence

Confidence, or lack of it, is the word that most regularly crops up in relation to women who want to return to work. Many people, but especially women, feel a lack of confidence in certain situations and those who have been out of paid employment for some time are often prone to such feelings. There are many social, economic and psychological reasons for lack of confidence that can't really be dealt with here. We hope that the exercises above have helped you to re-evaluate yourself and your position, your strengths and your weaknesses, and that, as a result, you are beginning to feel more sure of yourself. You may have been able to put past mistakes and failures into perspective and to put them behind you instead of letting them drag you down and using them as excuses for not changing or doing anything different. You may have discovered that things you have done are not necessarily run-of-the-mill and mundane but are actually achievements and show considerable ability and skill. An important thing to remember at any stage in life is that we learn from our mistakes. If we didn't make any, we wouldn't learn and develop as people.

Confidence can be developed but you have to practise and work at it. You have to turn negative thoughts into positive ones and banish excuses like 'It was my mother's fault I didn't do such and such when I was younger', and turn vague longings into action. Remember, if you don't have confidence in yourself you are hardly likely to inspire other people to have confidence in you. With more of an idea of who you are, your personality and abilities, you should be in a better position to explore and understand your needs and aspirations.

Knowing what you want is sometimes hard to pin down and it is easy to go along with what other people want and not be too demanding or assert your own needs. Assertion is a word that we hear quite often these days, in relation both to work and to social life generally. Assertiveness training courses have become very popular, especially with women, because they offer a range of techniques to help overcome passive or aggressive behaviour. Learning to be assertive can help someone to become more open and relaxed and increase self-confidence and control over one's life. You will probably find assertiveness courses on offer through your local adult or continuing education centre. Some large organizations also run courses for their employees. There are several books on the subject, the most well-known being *A Woman in Your Own Right*, by Anne Dickson (1982).

The trouble with becoming an assertive woman is that it takes time and practice. It's not something that you can expect to achieve merely because you have been on a course or read a book about it. You have to live it and practise it in everyday encounters. And there will be lapses, times when you wished you had stated your needs more clearly, when you feel resentful because you agreed to do something for someone that you really didn't want to do, when you let someone walk all over you. But knowing assertion techniques can be very liberating, not just for you but for partners, children, friends, bosses and so on. You have to know yourself, know what you want and ask for it. You hardly have the right to complain if someone doesn't do what you want or give you what you want if you don't state clearly what exactly it is you *do* want. You have the right to be considered with respect as an intelligent, capable and equal human being, to state your needs, to express your feelings, to make mistakes, to ask for what you want. People respond with more respect to reasonable requests and uncluttered messages, and you gain confidence from acquiring a basic belief in yourself.

Being assertive

It is commonly assumed that being assertive is the same as being aggressive, hard-nosed and unfeminine. It is often confused with being overbearing, insensitive and selfish. Of course, a few people might think that a confident, independent person is hard-nosed because she doesn't conform to the feminine stereotype of a passive, pliable person constantly at everyone's beck and call. Being assertive means being a woman in your own right, responsible for yourself, able to refuse requests without feeling guilty or

ASSERTION TRAINING: SOME DEFINITIONS

Non-assertiveness means:
- having difficulty standing up for yourself;
- voluntarily relinquishing responsibility for yourself;
- inviting persecution by assuming the role of victim or martyr.

Aggressiveness means:
- standing up for your rights in such a way that the rights of others are violated in the process;
- being self-enhancing at the expense of putting down or humiliating others;
- using *manipulation* as an indirect form of aggression – including subterfuge, trickery, seduction and subtle forms of revenge.

Assertiveness means:
- being able to express your needs, preferences and feelings in a manner that is neither threatening nor punishing to others;
- being able to express your needs, preferences and feelings without undue fear or anxiety;
- being able to express your needs, preferences and feelings without violating the rights of others;
- direct, honest communication between individuals interacting equally and taking responsibility for themselves.

Assertion training is about you and how you use your own power – whether you give it away, whether you use it to violate others or whether you use it constructively and assertively. It is about learning about yourself as an *individual* – how you are now and how you can change your behaviour.

It is *not* about changing the behaviour of others, though a change in you may open up new choices for the people with whom you are interacting.

It is *not* about changing organizations or changing society. To achieve change at these levels the individual will need to join with others to develop appropriate strategies.

feeling that people won't like you for doing so.

An aggressive person usually behaves in an aggressive, over-bearing way because they feel insecure and lack self-esteem much like a passive type of person. They need to prove their superiority by putting other people down or 'winning' arguments. Faced with a threatening situation, they often 'attack' as a form of defence, leaving a trail of hurt and humiliated feelings behind. They feel no real confidence in just being themselves as an assert-ive person might.

Being assertive means accepting your own positive and negative qualities, not trying to be a superwoman and not having to put someone else down in order to feel comfortable. It means taking responsibility for yourself and your actions and drawing the line between your own and someone else's problems. An assertive woman does not need to make others feel guilty for not recog-nizing her needs. She can recognize her needs and ask openly and directly – even though she risks refusal. Refusal or rejection is never pleasant but if you are an assertive person you won't feel demolished by it. Self-esteem is anchored deep within and you are not dependent on the approval of others around you. Learning to be assertive will not make you uncaring, selfish and insensitive but will help you to set your own limits about who to care for and whose needs to put before your own.

It is important to remember that no one is to blame if you are an aggressive, passive or manipulative type of person – to recog-nize is not to blame. In the past each of us has learned to cope in the best way we could, given the circumstances at the time. Once we can let ourselves off the hook of feeling bad or guilty about our behaviour, we can begin to see choices and make changes in our lives.

One way to start trying out assertive techniques is to make a list of situations in which you would like to be more assertive. These can be taken from any area of your life, such as when you are out shopping, with your family, with neighbours, with friends, at work and so on. Next to each situation write down how you behave now. It may help to do this exercise with a group of friends.

However, it's one thing to talk and think about your behaviour and another to change it. The principal means of doing this in assertion training is role-playing. Role-playing may be difficult for you, you may find it embarrassing, but it is essential if you want to rehearse and practise what you want to say and do in a particular situation. Once you are involved in playing out your role you will feel much as you do in the real life situation – anxious, frightened, guilty, angry and so on. Experiencing these feelings at first hand will help you when you come to tackle the 'real life' problem. You can set up a role-play situation at home with a trusted friend, especially if you know someone who has some understanding of what assertiveness is about. It is probably better to start with a situation that is not too difficult or fraught and move on to more difficult problems, perhaps involving long-standing relationships. An easy situation might be one that involves taking shoddy goods back to a shop and asking for your money back; a hard one might be how you are going to tell your mother that you will not be spending Christmas with her this year. Only try being assertive for real when you feel ready and don't try to tackle difficult problems before you've had one or two successes with smaller ones; you may undo the positive effect of building your self-confidence.

Body language

There are many aspects of assertion training, such as expressing anger, saying 'no' to requests and dealing with compliments and criticism, which we have not mentioned here but which are dealt with in Anne Dickson's book, *A Woman In Your Own Right* (1982), and would be covered in an assertiveness course. However, we will touch briefly on an important but often unconscious part of our behaviour which is integral to assertion.

One of the basic principles of assertion is to speak out firmly and clearly. However, there is not much point in sending assertive verbal messages if they are undermined by what our body is doing, if, for example, it is communicating lack of confidence, uncertainty or hostility. We send messages through our posture, gestures, tone of voice and facial expression, and in the way we use the space around us. As Anne Dickson points out: 'As women . . . most of us have learned how to smile appealingly, to gesture coyly, to pout, to wheedle and coax with our entire bodies. These habits get in the way of assertive communication'. They can be unlearned.

The way you walk, stand or sit reveals quite a lot about your-

ASSERTION TRAINING: THE BROKEN RECORD TECHNIQUE IN USE

Three skills you need:

1 Decide what it is you want or feel, and say so specifically and directly.
2 Stick to your statement, repeating it, if necessary, over and over again.
3 Assertively deflect any response from the other person which might undermine your stance.

Don't get caught on:

- Manipulative bait
- Irrelevant logic
- Argumentative bait

Example

Selma:	I bought this cheese yesterday. When I got home and opened it, I found it was mouldy. I want my money back please.
Shopkeeper:	Nothing to do with me. I wasn't here yesterday. [Irrelevant logic]
Selma:	I bought it in this shop and as it is inedible I want my money back please.
Shopkeeper:	That sort of cheese is meant to be mouldy. If you don't like that sort of thing you shouldn't buy it. [Argumentative bait]
Selma:	I know what kind of cheese I buy. This is bad and I want my money back.
Shopkeeper:	Look, there's a queue of people waiting behind you. Please would you let them pass. It's not fair they should have to wait. [Manipulative bait]
Selma:	I can see that there are people behind me but I bought this cheese yesterday. It is inedible and I want my money back.
Shopkeeper:	Well, how much was it then? [in a resigned, unfriendly voice, but nevertheless he gives the money back]

(Example taken from Anne Dickson, *A Woman in Your Own Right – Assertiveness and You* (1982))

GETTING TO KNOW YOU

self. Do you shuffle into a room, hoping no one will notice you, or do you march in like a thunderbolt? Do you hold your head straight or cock it to one side? You have more chance of communicating a direct approach if you stand squarely or sit directly in front of someone and don't sidle up to them as if you were apologizing for being there.

Eye contact is an important aspect of communication, as you've probably realized when talking to someone who can't meet your gaze or has a shifty look. Your gaze can be relaxed and friendly or it can convey hostility and embarrassment. Being able to look someone in the eye (without staring at them) can reinforce an assertive message.

It has been calculated that women smile more than men, probably in an effort to be 'nice' and to be 'liked'. It can be a mark of servility and inequality. Many of us have been so conditioned to be nice and encouraged to be sweet, appealing and placatory that we hardly notice we are doing it. Most women will, even if they are angry with someone, smile because of their nervousness and inhibition about being angry. 'The automatic smile is really a non-verbal message saying "Please don't be angry with me" or "I don't want to appear nasty"!' (Anne Dickson, 1982). If you are saying you are hurt or angry with a smile on your face, you must expect people not to take you seriously. They are probably confused.

We have probably all encountered voices we don't particularly like. In some respects people can't do much about their voices. On the other hand, between the simpering 'little girl' voice and the foghorn, there is a balance. Anne Dickson suggests practising the higher and lower registers of the voice, breathing and relaxation to release the constriction of the throat and chest, and to take a deeper breath to project the voice more fully.

Some people have irritating gestures that they are barely aware of: twiddling hair, biting fingernails and fiddling with jewellery are examples and can give the impression of tension and nervousness. Once we become aware of them, we can do something about them. Major adjustments are not necessarily what is required. If you think you have a tendency to slouch, to talk too fast, to giggle a lot or to play with your hands or fingers, think about what kind of impression these habits give other people. If you think they are predominantly negative, try to keep them under control – breathing deeply, relaxing your hands, your body, your neck muscles and so on can work wonders and give you a greater sense of well-being and confidence.

Action plan

Finally, drawing up an 'action plan' can be very helpful. If you have followed some of the exercises in this chapter you will have a greater sense of self and of your achievements. But you may be still concerned about what actions need to be taken to achieve objectives. Planning is important because it helps to sort out your priorities and organize your time effectively, giving you confidence to take the next steps to achieve your aims. When you are drawing up your action plan, you might like to bear in mind the following things:

- start small and let it grow; avoid grand, unachievable goals;
- be realistic about time-scales – don't expect overnight changes;
- review progress; be prepared to revise plans.

In Figure 2 you will find an example of what an action plan can look like. You can base yours on this or design one for yourself.

One of the most satisfying things about having an action plan is that you can cross things off once they have been accomplished. It can increase your self-confidence to realize that you are making things happen.

The last section of this chapter reviews the idea of self-development.

Learning through experience and self-development

That which can be taught directly to another is relatively trivial, whereas things of significance can only be learned.

Remember when it comes down to it that you are the person who is responsible for your own learning and development. We remember far more from what we learn than from what we are taught. Self-development is not about the transmission of knowledge. Rather it is about people acquiring and developing their own expertise and direction and the capacity to learn from experience. It is about people becoming active agents, not passive

'MANAGING YOURSELF' ACTION PLAN

PERSONAL GOALS

SHORT-TERM (6 months – 1 year)	
LONG-TERM (3 – 5 years)	

ACTIONS

PRIORITY DEVELOPMENT AREA	OBJECTIVE	TIME-SCALE	HOW TO ACHIEVE IT

Figure 2 Example of an action plan

recipients; it is about realizing potential. It is about learning from experience through a process of 'doing' and 'reviewing' (Figure 3).

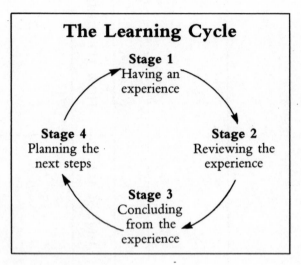

Figure 3 The learning cycle

If you have enough self-discipline, you could try to keep a learning log – a short written account of something that has occurred during an experience, a list of conclusions you have drawn from the experience or incident and a plan of action specifying what you are going to do in the light of your conclusions. In other words:

- reviewing the experience;
- concluding from the experience;
- planning the next steps.

You could write up your log, three times a week or once a week, but don't leave it lying around for weeks on end. You will lapse, but if you persevere you will find it easier to put into practice what you have learned from experience and map out the way ahead.

The final thing to say in this chapter is to urge you to recognize and *use* your potential: this will make you feel more confident and help you meet life's lucky breaks and its pitfalls in a positive way.

2

WOMEN TAKE CREDIT: ORGANIZATION OF PRIVATE LIFE

This chapter is all about organization. Even if you alter only one part of your life it will affect the rest to a greater or lesser extent. We need to control as much of our lives as possible, for having the feeling that we are out of control brings stress. It's true that often we can control only a proportion of the way we live and the decisions we make. Therefore it's all the more important to know what that proportion is, how we might increase it and the effects of our decisions upon it.

Jackie Brown felt rather annoyed at a quotation by George V, copied into her daughter's autograph book: 'The secret of life is not to do what you like but to try to like what you do.' So she wrote about it.

> o i do like ironing
> watching each pucker and wrinkle
> slide smooth from the iron's prow
> making tea-towels crumpled as unwanted letters
> into flat square parcels anyone
> would want the postman to bring
> o ironing is my favourite thing
>
> o and i do like washing
> the dishes after sunday dinner
> seeing grease clots glow among iridescent
> bubbles the plates emerge shiny
> as the newly converted
> baptised in the jordan
> o washing up banishes boredom

o and i really love scrubbing
the lavatory when the eldest's
been sick seeing the sun king enamel
come up gleaming as morning
and the loo blue making
a summer sky of the pan
o scrubbing the lavatory is fun

No doubt you can think up the content of several other stanzas. The dilemma is a real one, though. Can we change much? Do we have choices? Do we have to put up with liking what we do, with little hope of altering what we do? We can be creative and write a poem like Jackie but we can also consider other possibilities.

Many of the women who have been on New Opportunities for Women (NOW) or Fresh Start courses, when asked to give a reason why they've come, say they want to do something for themselves. They have felt pulled a number of ways, helping children, relatives, husband and friends and have forgotten themselves in the process. It is important that *you* consider what you want to do in the next five or ten years of your life.

First of all, consider the factors that will help towards change and which you can have some control over and then consider those that are beyond your control. In Figure 4 there are two

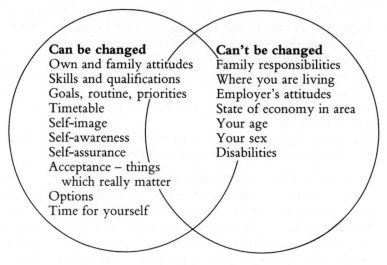

Can be changed
Own and family attitudes
Skills and qualifications
Goals, routine, priorities
Timetable
Self-image
Self-awareness
Self-assurance
Acceptance – things
  which really matter
Options
Time for yourself

Can't be changed
Family responsibilities
Where you are living
Employer's attitudes
State of economy in area
Your age
Your sex
Disabilities

Figure 4 Factors that can and cannot be changed

27

lists to start you off which have been put together by ex-NOW students. One of our major aims must be keep the first circle as large as possible and not to be overwhelmed by the second circle. Draw yet another circle and shade in the percentage of what can be changed at this moment in your life. Certainly don't let that proportion decrease.

Aims and objectives

You can sit down straight away with a friend and discuss your list of aims but usually it needs some thought and consideration. At this point we are concerned with the totality of your life so your aims should reflect all the interests in your life. In other chapters of this book your aims will be concentrated on getting back into paid work, on employment perspectives or educational qualifications and how to get them. Here is a general list compiled by Felicity Skelton.

Five-year aims
Staying sane.

Bringing up a child – instilling in her an appreciation of good literature, good music (including classical music) and lasting human values, i.e. acting as a counterpoint to the fast food, pop culture and superficiality with which she is surrounded.

Helping to get the Labour Party elected to government – and to carry out their policies and be electable a second time.

To finally *write* something.

To be more active in putting socialist and Christian values into practice.

To do *something* about Cambodia, El Salvador, Eritrea, etc.

To visit Russia.

To consider applying for directing work in professional theatre.

To encourage husband to find more acting work.

Some of the aims are obviously easier to achieve than others, but they add up to an interesting five years. You may wish to include some short-term aims as well as mid- and long-term ones, and think of a fair sprinkling of ones which you can reasonably achieve. It's a good idea to have a few notions about what you would do if absolutely nothing barred the way, but a complete list organized on this basis would be depressing reading after a few months when you might not have accomplished any of them by then.

As a version of this exercise, imagine yourself five or ten years ahead when your plans have been successful. What would you be able to say? Or suppose you are writing a script for a play or a film about someone exactly like yourself. Write the next few scenes. What would you want this character to do? This exercise is quite useful at distancing yourself from your present situation.

We have to make choices and balance our responsibilities, so let us be positive about it. Keep your overall aims in review and look at them every six months or so. A collection over a few years makes a very interesting kind of diary!

You may want to consider several aspects of your life in your list: family, work, education, recreation, artistic expression – anything from embroidery to photography. It is very difficult to get everything accomplished without a list and most women are excellent list-makers.

Prioritizing or managing time

The next exercise was first constructed for people who work in very busy offices with the phone ringing and plenty of interruptions. But it is of great use in many and varied situations.

Make two lists: what you expect and need to do (a) in the next week and (b) tomorrow. Then take the lists and label the items A, B or C in level of importance. You can then look at the A items, and label them A1, A2, A3. Discuss this list in small groups or with a friend to consider what you do or don't give importance to. Here are Felicity's lists.

Week's list
Type out School Governors' statement for meeting.
Find costume for child for Christmas concert.
Bring books up to date and prepare VAT returns.
Buy and send off Christmas presents for family abroad.
Do a mountain of ironing.
Book car in for conversion to unleaded petrol.
Sew buttons on various people's clothes, including my own.
Start knitting woollies for child.
Finish typing and send off letter re Cambodia to the Prime Minister.
Make cakes for tea-shop.

Tomorrow's list

A Baking for tea-shop.

A Make shopping list for husband and send him off as soon as possible so I can get on with baking.

A Get guest rooms changed and cleaned.

A Get child up, dressed, fed and down to school.

C Finish letter to the Prime Minister.

C Ring mother.

B Be nice to husband when he comes home and help unpack car and put shopping away.

B Be nice to stepson.

C Get child into bed *earlier*. Give her a bath, if time.

C Wash my hair.

C Have a bath.

Felicity has a busy life and has not listed anything much concerned with her long-term aims as an A job for tomorrow. Have you? Or are the A items entirely concerned with shopping, collecting the children from school, visiting a friend in hospital, etc.? All very important and necessary, but somewhere as well you should have something about looking for job advertisements, reading a prospectus, making a specific contact, or finding out information to help you implement your aims.

Never think 'I'll get rid of the C's first and then get down to the important things.' That way you feel frustrated, your energy gets dissipated and you don't gain a sense of achievement. Tackle the A's first.

Some of your A items may be rather overwhelming or disagreeable, for example actually getting down to applying for a job, or doing out the back bedroom because you have someone coming to stay and it's in a right mess. It is a cardinal virtue always to do such things first. Deadlines help. If you have to get something done by tomorrow you usually can, and you feel fantastically pleased with yourself when you do. Just think back over your life and the multiplicity of things you have accomplished. Think of your work autobiography (if and when you've written one) and you will realize you have already achieved a great deal, and will go on to achieve more.

Case study

This is a case study which indicates the difficulties involved in studying but also how determination can get you a long way.

Jacky Fisher left school with no qualifications. Although she wanted to be a teacher, she'd had a part-time job in a hairdresser's and her family expected her to take that up as a full-time career. She gained a distinction in City and Guilds Hairdressing before marrying and having two children. She still wanted to be a teacher, though.

My daughter started at comprehensive school and the Head invited parents into school to take examinations if they wished. The head of sixth form was less helpful when I said I wanted to take Maths GCE. *He* implied that I couldn't possibly achieve this as I had left school so long ago. He suggested I take Computer Studies and if I was successful then he would reconsider.

I gained a B in Computer Studies and English Language that summer and the next year English Literature, Biology and Maths. I postponed my studies for a while because my father was terminally ill but I did attend a New Opportunities course. Following that I went to a Mature Matriculation course at Sheffield University, where I enjoyed the lectures but these occurred during the evening and since the premises were very near the 'red light' district I was frightened of going home by myself at 10.30 p.m. In June that year my son, Andrew, had a severe accident and was in hospital for three weeks. I was at hospital continuously and with exams coming up I decided to withdraw.

The next year I enrolled for A Levels in English and Psychology. This meant part-time study of three half-days a week and one evening. I also applied to Sheffield Polytechnic to become a student on the B.Ed. course — at 36 years old. I knew so much depended on the exams, I was a nervous wreck. By the end of my first English paper I walked out in tears, I had made a mess of it. The pressure was terrible. My results, to me, were disastrous. English a fail (N), Psychology B. But I was accepted by the Poly two weeks before term started and I am now in year three of the course.

My children were very supportive at first, perhaps my daughter found it quite amusing. Then, when she was taking GCEs I was on A Levels – not good timing. I think Helen viewed me as being in competition with her. I had become a single parent and both children at times got fed up with me sitting in one room for very long periods studying. On one occasion my daughter actually asked me to give it all up. This hurt but I was sure I had to continue because they would grow up and leave home and I still have a right to my own life. I feel now that they are both proud of me and Andrew is always eager to tell everyone, 'My mum is going to be a teacher.'

At times I cannot deny I have felt utter desperation, feeling so unsure about the amount of time spent studying, feeling absolutely isolated because studying is often something you can only do on your own. I have felt very irresponsible when I've missed lectures because of my children's illnesses. You can't wear your heart on your sleeve but the problems of bringing up a family and studying, especially at degree level, should not be underestimated. However, the satisfaction gained when you're successful tends to outweigh the bad times. It also gives me a sense of identity. I feel much more confident than I did five years ago.

My daughter was very successful at school and Andrew seems to be following in her footsteps. I feel sure that my own interest in education has had positive effects on them. I have no regrets at all about my decision.

You may feel you just can't face tackling something because it is rather frightening or you've put it off for so long you don't know where to start or because it needs hours of 'serious' work and you never have enough time to get down to it. Then give yourself time to think about it – say, ten minutes. One woman had put off writing her MA thesis for so long it became threatening even to contemplate her great quantity of notes, let alone start putting any of them together. It began to seem as if she would never complete her degree. Eventually she decided how much time she could bear thinking about it – two minutes! During that two minutes she began to consider what she could do; she'd made a start. The next day she was able to spend longer on it and indeed soon got into a working pattern again. Ten minutes is a more reasonable span of time, perhaps. You can achieve something, make a beginning and anyone can stand ten minutes. It's surprising how often you find that if you start off with ten minutes you actually find you can bear to spend thirty minutes or an hour on the problem.

One student told us she wrote things on a list in order to cross them off: a harmless enough occupation but most of us have more things to put on a list than we can cope with!

You may want to juggle items from A to C or vice versa. Washing the kitchen ceiling may be a C item now but perhaps in six months when it still hasn't been cleaned you may promote it to A. Select the important items and concentrate on them. No one can do everything, everyone can achieve a great deal.

Co-operation

Richard Leakey, who for many years has studied the origins of the human race, has suggested that it is co-operation which has ensured our survival. Women are particularly good at co-operation, as evidenced through centuries of mutual child care, communal washing arrangements, wood-gathering or 'sticking parties'. We also show this through linguistic practice, in that we tend to listen to each other without always trying to compete for talking space. Most of the caring for dependants is taken on by women and much of the communal fund-raising for educational and hospital projects is done by women. As someone once said, 'If you had to have bring-and-buy parties to purchase a battleship or an airforce fighter, how many ships or planes would we have?'

Co-operation is a useful, even vital, feature of our life. It is marketable, in terms of potential employers (emphasize the various ventures in which *you* have co-operated, worked as part of a team), but also can, and often must be nurtured.

How are you going to manage with all the extra pressures of a new job, training or several hours of studying added on to the work you already do? Encourage a sense of co-operation among those who live with you. This probably means several discussions or 'meetings' on the issue. This in itself is probably good, since usually we don't give enough time over to discussion of family affairs – we just wait till it all blows up. See if general chores can be divided up, devise rotas for cleaning and cooking – though always bear in mind what is possible as well as what is scrupulously equal. It is a great help to have every member of the household take charge of cooking one meal a week and, although it might be fairer for them to cook twice, will it be worth the organization and the hassle? Certainly there must be a definite level of co-operation (don't let people 'help' with the washing up!) but consider what is the best balance.

Work out how often the bathroom needs cleaning (allegedly one of the tasks *always* left to females), the kitchen floor washing and any other essential jobs. They are A on the weekly list, while others can be put into the C category, at least for the time being. It is often helpful to design a week's menu with some consultation. We had sausages once a week for several months at a stretch because the youngest member of the household only wanted to cook sausages, and we couldn't impose a three-course cordon bleu meal on him. Place the menu on the wall. Often people will start helping with a meal, for instance cutting up vegetables, if they know that it is going to be shepherd's pie or spaghetti bolognaise or nutloaf. It is the blank of not knowing, of having to *think* of a meal, that often prevents people helping. Thinking up the menu in advance is half the battle. Cooking can become one of the pleasant communal activities in your house – so you may need to buy extra chopping-boards and more than one vegetable peeler. It is better to have more 'organized' co-operation than to rely on frozen food, and much healthier too.

Other people around you need to be involved in more than domestic chores. There is some evidence to show that further study or career promotion for a woman can lead to problems within a partnership. This is a chicken-and-egg question of course, since the relationship might have been teetering before one partner moved into a new area. It is likely, however, that plenty of discussion will help rather than hinder matters. Discussion about what you're doing, reading and learning. And listening.

Counselling or advisory services exist for working co-operatives just as more orthodox businesses can bring in consultant trouble-shooters. Such counselling groups have discovered that, more often than not, difficulties arise because people are not listening to each other. Listening and taking note of others' opinions is an advanced skill. We might expect our children to listen to us but often do not present them with a model which they can imitate.

Listening and counselling exercise

You need to do this in pairs and to be able to trust the other person. Decide in advance what you are both going to talk about. It is a useful exercise for people in relationships talking over one problem, but two individuals can talk about what is worrying them separately. Then give each other equal time, perhaps between fifteen and twenty minutes each. Sit in 'equal' positions, for example either both on the floor or in chairs of the same height. You may hold hands if you feel this is appropriate. Have a watch or a clock with you. One person talks from their point of view for the fifteen or twenty minutes and then the situation is changed and the other person takes over. Don't interrupt but you can ask helpful questions. Don't worry if there is a minute or two of silence. Give complete attention to the speaker. If you are talking over the same problem you may want to exchange views now, having listened to each other. Or to have a general conversation on the two problems. It often clarifies matters for the speaker as well as the listener. Completing this exercise makes you aware how seldom we listen properly to other people's points of view.

Control of life-style

Think about what you want in your life, how you can maximize the benefits of working with the pleasures of life at home, with friends and family. It would probably be an excellent idea (at least for two-thirds of our readers) if you added some physical recreation to your list of aims. Apparently only one-third of women (compared with over half of men) regularly attend a leisure centre or engage in sport. The Sports Council is on record as stating that this may be due to a lack of free time! Plenty of women have found they can run full marathons, and, although you might not wish to be quite so energetic, some jogging, swimming or yoga might well make you feel better emotionally and physically. Try out a number of sports. If it's a long time since you have done any sport, or can remember only too well raw, cold days playing hockey at school, you may not enjoy the first few times you go to a leisure centre, or the first choice you make. The fact that you find you dislike badminton doesn't mean you won't like anything else, such as fencing or aerobics or yoga. Find someone else who's hesitant and decide to go swimming or running together.

Money

You may think you spend a great deal of time worrying about money but, even so, begin thinking a little further. Probably everyone knows by now the statement in the United Nations Report: 'Women constitute half the world's population, perform nearly two-thirds of its work hours, receive one-tenth of the world's income and own less than one-hundredth of the world's property.' You might not feel quite so exploited as this maintains but at least be in control of what you have. Unfortunately there are still women, widowed in their seventies, who never signed a cheque when their husbands were alive or dealt with any of the larger financial transactions in the family. No doubt they managed their housekeeping budget superbly, but that didn't give them sufficient training for dealing with all their financial dealings later.

Being in control means more discussions (not again, you may say!), with everyone concerned, on priorities in spending. It means taking advice from knowledgeable people, whether the problem concerns pensions, benefits, tax or paying back debts. It is heartening to read about some women who, ensnared into a mounting debt spiral by persuasive loan sharks, have started self-help groups to reduce dependence on such illusory methods of escape. Women are often poor because they are single parents. Thirteen per cent of all families, that is more than one in eight, have a single woman at their head. If you are in this position it is worth finding out from your local Gingerbread Group or Citizen's Advice Bureau exactly what your financial rights are. And keep asking about such matters, because the rules keep changing.

Financial details of your own budget are difficult to discuss in groups, since as a society we get quite anxious about our financial status. However, here is one good exercise: decide in small groups or pairs which areas of financial advice would benefit you and contact those organizations or read relevant pamphlets before your next meeting (or make a definite date to do so). Apart from anything else this procedure will help you gain confidence in your ability to find information and talk to people about items of concern to you. It will certainly help in your training for interviews.

Child care

The proportion of married women in the work-force increases each year (see Figure 9, p. 147) and many of them face difficulties over child care. So far there are few options: nurseries, childminders and nannies. Employers are now considering work-based nurseries. For example, Midland Bank has estimated the cost of replacing the 1,100 women they lose per year for child-care reasons at between fifteen and twenty million pounds. They have begun establishing nurseries at or near the mother's place of work since they need married women to return as part of their work-force. At the moment these are few and far between but are likely to increase. However, work-place nurseries can tie you to a particular job since it is difficult to move jobs and leave the child care as it was. Local Authority nurseries exist but are under enormous pressure for places and can often only help families with needs other than those concerned with parents' employment. In 1985 61 per cent of mothers with children of 3 years and under were not doing paid work of any kind. This is hardly surprising since Local Authority day nurseries have approximately 33,000 places for 0–4-year-olds, which is about 1 per cent of all children under 5.

Child-minders are an option for many mothers. You will need to build in time to liaise with your child-minder and see that the relationship with your child or children is working well. You will also need to look at your budget beforehand to consider the financial implications of working, child care and travel. It may be that you will decide to work for a very small return for some years so that you can continue in your work, keep up to date with what's happening, and have an eye to promotion. Looking after children is quite clearly a tremendously important human activity (unfortunately not yet recognized by any of our governments) and you won't want to pay the person looking after your child at a very low rate.

One other problem concerns the easing of children into the education system. The number of hours your child will need nursery-type care will lessen, but gradually, and over a period of years if you have two or three children. This may cause employment problems in terms of retaining the same child-minder or nanny. You need to consider and discuss the situation before it arises.

Case study

One group in London decided to set up their own child-care facilities. It was and is extremely hard work but got them what they wanted for their children and proved what excellent organizers, managers and co-operators they must be. **Kathryn James** writes:

The nursery was started by four women who had had babies within two months of each other and who either needed to find some child care for when they returned to work or wanted some other kind of child-care arrangement. One woman noticed a library Hackney Council was turning into a community centre. Last April we were promised a small room in the centre about 12' × 25' for our use temporarily and shared use of the large main hall and kitchen. We're still there! We spent several weeks fund-raising, buying toys (mostly second-hand) and meeting to discuss finances, workers and policy. We decorated, laid carpet, painted, made things safe. We advertised and introduced three new sets of parents and babies, which were no problem to find, and we also advertised and employed a NNEB full-time worker. Some parents worked at the nursery and were paid for that and it was one way to offset the cost of when their babies were there on other days. We also took on some part-time workers.

We eventually opened the nursery on 19 June 1989, Monday-Friday 8.30–5, with fees of £12 per day. We try to have no more than three babies per worker at any one time, which I don't think we ever have but sometimes parents have to cover so that the ratio of worker to babies is kept that low. The rotas for workers and the pay are very complicated. At the moment we have never more than seven babies there at one time, which in theory creates an income of 7 × 12 = £84 per day = £420 per week. We employed one full-time worker from 8.30 to 4.30, who is paid £122 per week and £15 lunch allowance, two part-time workers from 9 to 1 and 1 to 5 at £3 per hour and a trainee on £35 per week training allowance. We top up her wage by £20 per week. She does PPA courses on two days so we pay a parent to come in at lunch-time on those days so the full-time worker can go to lunch. The workers have one hour for lunch, four weeks' paid holiday per year (the nursery closes for one week at Christmas, Easter and summer and they have another week) and two weeks' paid sick-leave per year. Our income has to cover extra workers at holidays and sick-leave. It also covers heating costs, equipment (paint, paper, etc.) and sundries like cotton wool, tea and coffee.

Parents provide cover from 8.30 to 9 and 4.30 to 5 on a rota. They also provide lunch, cleaning and sick cover on rotas. Each parent has a role within the group. Mine is administrator of all rotas; others include treasurer, research into and purchase of major equipment like climbing-frames, etc. We meet every other Wednesday evening to discuss issues and business.

We aim to provide a safe and secure environment for our children to play and grow in an anti-racist, anti-sexist nursery. The food we provide is vegetarian and as far as possible sugar- and salt-free. We aim to use our anti-sexist and anti-racist principles in our recruitment of babies and workers. Where women who have babies apply for jobs we try to accommodate a nursery place for their child.

Some of the positive things that have come out of the group are:

1 A small core of babies (now ten) who are all within 10 months of age where they are beginning to relate to each other (1 year to 22 months) and know each other's parents. They all receive a lot of attention because of the good ratios and all the babies seem genuinely very happy there. And very safe.
2 A sense of achievement and confidence at setting up a nursery. It's amazing what resources there are among parents.
3 People your child knows well for baby-sitting, which is indispensable in the absence of an extended family!

Some problems that occur running a parent-organized nursery:

1 Time and energy – if you work and have a child time is precious and it can be gruelling to spend evenings or weekends cooking, cleaning or on the phone arranging rotas.
2 We share the hall with other user groups whose needs and standards aren't compatible with ours – they smoke, sometimes break windows. The last thing you want to do at 8 a.m. on a Monday morning before work is put the vacuum cleaner around a community centre.
3 We are threatened with being chucked out of the centre at any time. We are trying to find alternative premises.
4 Perhaps because the fees are quite high (although the going rate for a private nursery in London) we haven't been able to attract babies and parents of black or ethnic minority origin. This is something we really have to tackle and perhaps might approach cultural organizations to see if they are prepared to subsidize places.

A final point: interviewers often ask questions about child care, whether they should or not. You can reply angrily and ask if they question male applicants in the same way. Probably you will be better off saying calmly that you have given the matter considerable thought as it is of great importance to you, and have organized everything quite satisfactorily to fit in with the hours advertised in the job.

Contacts

We often hear talk of 'Old Boy' networks, 'golf' friendships and business contacts in the bar or club. Women are often excluded from these, either because they didn't go to school with the 'Old Boys' or because they don't have time for as many recreational pastimes. Perhaps there might also be some hesitancy among some women at any suggestion they might be 'using' their friends. 'Using' means exploiting and no one is suggesting that. But all through this chapter (and indeed the book) we have emphasized discussion and seeking information and advice. The more people you know from whom you can get information and with whom you can discuss problems, job intentions, travel plans, child care, depression or interview experiences, or anything come to that, the better. Maximize your potential and theirs. Of course, reciprocity is implicit. You would be expected to respond in similar ways, if requested.

Exercise Write down as many people as you can whom you could contact for specific information or to talk over matters of mutual concern. This includes close friends and relatives. You should have a list of about fifty when you've thought about it over several days. Some people reach 200 quite easily. Keep updating the list and try to add names for the areas of interest to you in the near future.

Do not fall into the trap of undervaluing women's groups because they are women's groups and therefore don't have the pre-eminence in our society that they deserve. The Women's Institute, the National Housewives' Register, various support groups such as Women in Engineering and more informal groups have immense expertise and commitment in their specific areas. Include them in your network of helpful associations. Many self-help groups (for example the Playgroups' Association, various child illness and victim support groups and Tenants' Associations) have been begun by women. If there is no group to help you in your immediate locality, why not start one? The Playgroups Association and a league of women voters in Australia began by letters in a newspaper. You could send a letter to a national or local paper or put a postcard up in a local shop or just invite a group round to your house. Networking works.

Stress

Stress is a natural part of life and unless we are unusually fortunate we will not be able to avoid it for long periods of time. Some people say that it would not be good for us if we did, that stress proves our capabilities and enables us to achieve more than we would without it. However, even though we might agree with Mae West that too much of a good thing can be very nice, no one wants too much stress. Research carried out in 1980 seems to indicate that women managers are subjected to a greater number of work-related pressures compared with their male counterparts. It is reasonable to believe that a cross-comparison of any job would lead to the same conclusion. Add to that the fact that women with children have to cope with a dual role, and that, although there are many sympathetic men around, apparently most women still consider that they do more housework and child care than their partner, so it would seem inevitable that women are under more stress.

The main sources of stress at work come from work overload, the feeling of being undervalued and therefore not being given enough demanding work, or being the boss and having to acquire male managerial skills such as assertiveness. Women often overload themselves, on the basis that they have to be seen to be good at their job and often have to be better than a male colleague in a similar position if they wish to be promoted at the same time. It is likely that women who try to cope by meeting the demands of all their multiple roles (wife, mother, worker) by becoming a 'superwoman' are those most at risk in relation to stress-related illnesses.

Coronary disease is frequently used as a statistical sign of the frequency of stress in particular groups. Research has shown that the incidence of coronary heart disease among working women rose as the number of children increased. The reverse was true of housewives – a slight decrease was shown with more children.

Other indicators show similar trends. Adjustment in marriage or other partnerships seems to be more difficult for dual-career women (that is, women who go out to work and have family responsibilities) than for women who do not have paid employment when they also have child-care requirements to meet. Treatment for alcoholism has doubled for men in recent years but trebled for women. Also, differences are shown in the way men and women use smoking. Men tend to smoke when they are relaxing, women when they are going through a period of stress.

Given the probability that a new job will bring extra stress (particularly when coupled with domestic duties), do look out for any symptoms; for example, continual bouts of tiredness, depression or irritability or trouble with sleeping. Everyone reacts differently under pressure so it is important to discover what exactly it is in your environment that is stressful. Along with all your other lists it may be useful to keep a stress diary for a few weeks. Write down at the end of each day what was or were the most stressful incidents of the day (e.g. confronting a particular colleague) or series of incidents (e.g. phone interruptions). If you know what causes you particular problems, you can try to develop some coping strategies.

You may need to have some assertiveness training to cope with problems at work. Such courses are run in community education centres, in management centres and by some firms as part of their in-house training. When outside your paid employment you may need to develop relaxation techniques, set aside more time for yourself, which might well include physical recreation, or look for counsellors, either in a counselling group or professionally. You may want to attend one of the many relaxation courses on offer, including yoga and various meditation techniques. You can follow exercises in a group or by yourself from a book such as *In Our Own Hands: A Book of Self-help Therapy*, by Sheila Ernst and Lucy Goodison (1981). Relaxation needs organizing just as much as work does, if you wish to lead a balanced life. The more well-adjusted you are, the better you can cope.

3

SPEAKING AND WRITING: WOMEN AND LANGUAGE

As a starter to this chapter consider first how important you think language is and secondly how you would define 'language'. Many people use words such as 'vital' or 'essential' in answer to the first question and, for the second, arrive at a number of definitions (it is impossible to have just one) which embrace communication, behaviour and a sense of identity. Perhaps you will include other qualities in your definition of language but you will almost certainly agree on its overwhelming importance to us all. This is why we have included a chapter which looks at language by way of two skills: speaking and writing. It is important that we communicate clearly and effectively with each other, that we know how and why we speak as we do, and that we encourage a justifiable sense of pride in *our* language, whatever it is and whatever dialect we speak.

Girls grow up with a definite advantage in verbal skills. At birth they are more developed physically than male babies and so they can focus clearly on a face earlier than boys do, as well as being able to distinguish individual sounds. This advantage carries on through the early years and may have been one reason why more girls than boys used to pass the eleven-plus (although this generally went unnoticed because the numbers involved were 'equalized' by the education authorities). Far more girls than boys study English at A Level and degree level but it is not considered a 'vocational' or 'professional' qualification so does not benefit girls in quite the way one might imagine.

Girls do not speak as much as boys in school just as women do not speak as much as men. They do not ask questions or volunteer information or gain the teacher's attention as frequently

45

as boys do. So why don't we make better use of our verbal skills? There are complex sociological and psychological answers to that question; if you wish to go into the subject more deeply, do look up some of the books in the Reading List. At the moment we're concerned to change matters so that women *are* encouraged to speak out more boldly and self-confidently.

First of all decide at what stage you are in terms of the following list and what point you want to get to:

1 able to participate effectively in discussions of two or three people;
2 able to participate effectively in discussions of six or seven people;
3 able to give a brief prepared commentary, perhaps introduce a topic for discussion to groups of between six and fifteen, usually people you know;
4 able to contribute effectively to a formal meeting of fifteen or over;
5 able to ask questions or make points at a fairly large, open meeting;
6 able to give a speech to a group or meeting consisting of people you don't know.

The list is intended to indicate a sense of development but individuals may well differ: for example, someone may be able to put forward questions effectively at a large meeting but still worry about giving a brief commentary to five or six people.

It is difficult to consider speaking except in a group context. If you are at home reading this, perhaps you can arrange to get together with other women to try out the exercises and discuss the issues involved. You can disregard the sections where you feel quite competent.

Small groups

It is much easier to speak in smaller groups than larger ones, so if you are nervous about speaking in public begin with a small group. Many women suffer from the feeling that they have nothing worth saying. They are only housewives, or only talk to young children most of the time, or haven't been educated very much, or if they have then it was years ago, and so on. There is no lack of excuses. You can rid yourself, to some extent, of the fear of speaking, by listening to other women talking. Most women in groups feel that they have little to offer individually but that everyone else sounds all right. Follow that to its logical conclusion: if everyone thinks everyone else talks reasonably well, then *everyone* does. And that includes you.

A listening exercise: do this preferably in pairs, though you can manage with three people. This is slightly more difficult than the ice-breaking suggestion in Chapter One but follows along the same lines. One of you talks for a limited time, say between eight and ten minutes. Pick a topic which everyone knows about and/or has opinions concerning. 'Sex differences' is quite a good topic. Everyone knows what she thinks *are* sex differences, learnt or biological, and has examples of situations where these differences are apparent and opinions about them. As the person speaks the other notes down what she says. It may be necessary to help the conversation along with 'mmm', 'oh dear' and other such minimal responses, but do not ask leading questions or contradict anything, even if you disagree vehemently (or even slightly) with what has been said.

Change over roles and repeat activity. Subsequently, if you are members of a larger group you can report on what your partner said. If there are just two of you, repeat to the other what you think she said and see if she agrees. Such an activity reinforces a number of skills. It is easier speaking on a one-to-one basis. Any hesitations (and there will be some) or repetitions, or times when your thoughts appear a little muddled, won't matter. From the point of view of the listener, you will be surprised to find out how difficult it is to listen attentively. It is also a good beginning to talking to a larger group, since all you are doing is reporting someone else's ideas and trying to represent them sincerely.

Jigsaws

This begins with small groups but can involve larger groups if you wish. Then you can practise several strategies at once. In a small group of three or four (no more), discuss a particular item on an agenda or in a report. Other groups will discuss the same or similar topics. After ten or twenty minutes change groups. It is then your role within a new group to explain what your group discussed and what their conclusions were, and also to listen to the other people give their reports. This makes a reporting back session much more interesting as far more people are involved.

Talking within a larger group

This can be daunting even if only six or seven people are present. (Of course, this does depend on how well you know the people.) If you feel uneasy, think of something you *can* say. It is nearly always possible to state, 'I agree with what —— said', or 'that was a good point'. Usually you don't have to add anything and one person at least will feel well disposed towards you.

It has been noted that people are much more likely to speak once they have spoken. This may not seem much help if you are shy or feel inarticulate, but does make sense. The more confidence you have, the more you are able to speak. Some old advice suggests looking at the windows in the room where you are. If they are open ask for one to be shut, if they are closed ask for one to be opened. The idea is that you've broken the ice, you've spoken, now you can go on to say something more interesting. The point is a good one. Try to say something fairly early on in the discussion, maybe just an indication of agreement, and then you will speak more easily afterwards.

It also makes us feel more confident if we help others enter a discussion. So if you see someone trying to break into a conversation but another person always manages to speak a couple of seconds before, say something like: 'I think Helen has a point to make.' Then you'll both have achieved a statement.

Reading aloud

An interesting and simple way of addressing a few people is to read out a few paragraphs from something you have written as a group topic. 'Short talks' can become a little boring and something of a false situation if fifteen people get up one after the other and describe their hobbies, however interesting they may be. But if you have all written on some topic of interest to you as a group, such as education, marriage, single parenting, old age, women's health, depression, previous work experience – all topics that have been chosen by groups in the past – then it is useful to read out a few paragraphs from what you have written. You probably won't have time to read everything. Reading like this is not as easy as it sounds, but it achieves one important end – *ownership* of opinion. It is one thing to sit at home and scribble down a few ideas and quite another to give vent to them in discussion and accept ownership of them. Such reading aloud can be very rewarding when accomplished in a situation of mutual support and interest (and groups *are* supportive). Writing and talking on one topic stimulates discussion and allows exploration of a variety of points of view. The situation is also more comparable to that of a conversation, where we develop each other's contribution rather than begin on a totally new topic with each speaker.

You may wish to add a second stage to the exercise and ask people to stand up when they read their pieces out. It is amazing how different, and at first, how vulnerable, you feel. Not only are you speaking but you are visibly the centre of attention. On the other hand, it is often much easier to project your voice more clearly if you are standing and it is definitely easier for the listeners. Certainly women have told us that such exercises have helped them make comments at occasions such as parents' evenings at their children's school.

Meetings

Our bodies go through a number of physiological changes when we ask questions or raise points in a fairly large group of people. One noticeable effect is the increased heart rate. Everyone suffers from this so it isn't just you. There may be other symptoms also, blushing for instance. It is worth remembering that these body changes *will* occur and we should therefore try to be prepared for them. The only way to lessen their effects is to speak more often. What is particularly annoying is to get all psyched up to make a point and then someone else makes it and you have to sit still, your body rumbling to a state of accommodation. Sometimes that happens because you haven't the courage to get in and make the point. At least indicate agreement that the point should be raised – not all of us are able or willing to say 'hear, hear' except ironically, but the phrase has a function. It shows agreement – so why not say instead 'Yes, indeed' or 'I'm glad that's been asked'? And then your higher pulse rate has not been in vain.

You may need to sit through one or two meetings to find out how they are organized. Although there are general rules for organized meetings, the way the meeting is chaired can affect the proceedings; some follow rules much more rigidly than others. Note how other members of the meeting gain the attention of the chair, so that you can follow suit. A good chairperson will be looking for contributors – it may need only a glance and a nod, or in larger meetings you may need to raise your hand. If you have time, read all the relevant papers beforehand so that you know on which items you may wish to comment.

Women tend to become more involved in public meetings as they grow older, through parents' associations, school governing bodies, community associations, self-help groups and career organizations. It is likely that sometime you *will* need the skills to become involved in meetings or committee work. Don't let the structure of meetings confuse you. First concentrate on raising your confidence about speaking. You don't have to speak at every meeting but you aren't fully participating if you *never* express an opinion or offer information.

Making a point at a meeting

This is in fact quite difficult. It is particularly important to catch the eye of whoever is chairing the meeting. If you know beforehand that you are going to raise a point, then find a fairly conspicuous situation opposite the chair. The larger the meeting (over fifteen or so) the louder you will need to speak.

Remember that your pulse rate will increase, you will begin to feel warmer and your hands may sweat as your body prepares for the occasion. Try to enter the discussion quickly once the issue comes up, but don't be despondent if other people speak first. You may have to put your hand up several times or signal in some other way to the chair, before you are successful.

To give you confidence, try to rally some support beforehand. Then you'll know when you make the point or ask the question there will be at least some murmurs of agreement that the issue has been raised. You can offer such support to other speakers. Speaking in all forms is a communal activity so if we organize a group response we should not need to worry so much about our presentation, even though for a few seconds we might be standing up alone to make a statement.

Addressing a meeting

You may or may not wish to do this as a group exercise. Not everyone sees a need to develop this expertise, though it is surprising how people rise to the occasion. The women's support groups in the miners' strike of 1984 are an excellent example of confidence-raising. Women who had never spoken in public before found themselves addressing larger and larger audiences, sometimes upwards of a hundred, and occasionally abroad. However, this kind of activity does depend on your life-style and you may or may not be interested in talking to fairly large groups of people.

51

Speaking in public needs preparation, if only to give you confidence. Having written your speech try reading it out aloud a few times, preferably to a couple of sympathetic listeners. As far as possible you don't want to be reading it word for word on the actual occasion as you will want to look at your audience. So you should know it fairly well by then. Some speakers have a series of cards. This procedure has a number of beneficial results. As a speech-maker you will have to divide the talk into a number of separate units. This often helps the sequence and allows your audience a clearer understanding of how one item follows another. You also have a moment when you can look up at the end of each card and smile, or whatever you feel like doing, before you start the next one. Do have the cards numbered so that you don't get confused if, in a moment of aberration, you shuffle them into disorder. And remember that a pause or hesitancy may seem ages to you, but is likely to seem much less to the audience.

While you are waiting to speak on formal occasions concentrate on taking deep breaths so that when you do speak you sound calm and in control. Try to decide beforehand whether or not you will stand up to speak. It is easier to project your voice if you do. Look in the direction you wish your voice to travel and never at the floor or the top of a desk or table.

Most public speakers tell humorous anecdotes about the various horrific events that befell them on occasions when they were speaking. Actually such occurrences are few and far between but such anecdotes highlight the importance we attach to speaking and the corresponding worry that something may go wrong. The audience is composed of people like you, and you are reasonably supportive of the speaker (if not her ideas), aren't you?

Mixed-sex conversations and discussions

It sometimes seems almost as difficult if not so frightening to get your point across in conversation as in a large meeting. There are many misconceptions about language use and if we know about them this knowledge in turn helps us talk more effectively. Take interruptions, for example. No doubt, like us, you were brought up on the belief that interruptions were rude and impolite. Probably they are and it would be better if people did not interrupt each other, at least not frequently. But it is a researched fact that men interrupt a conversation more frequently than women do, and particularly if they are talking to a woman. So keep this information in mind. If you are interrupted particularly by one person state clearly that you want to finish your point. And don't let yourself be put down by being told (as we often are) that you're 'interrupting'. You probably aren't, and, even if you are, you most probably are much more often the victim than the interrupter so just keep on this once.

Some other useful knowledge to bear in mind:

- Men speak for longer periods and more frequently than women. Conversely, women are more silent.
- Men usually decide the subjects for discussion in mixed-sex conversation.
- Often women are consciously more concerned about the way they speak than men are.
- Women are more supportive in conversation, by encouraging other speakers to join in and by employing 'minimal responses', for example 'yes' and 'mmm'.

Since such differences in language use have developed along with the human capacity for speech it may seem impossible or undesirable for us to change. On the other hand if women wish to succeed in new kinds of employment or in different management positions and to take more effective control of their life-style, why not consider whether or not our newly acquired knowledge about language (all information about linguistic differences is very recent) can be of help? Apparently women prefer talking to other women but we live in a world where mixed-sex conversations are an essential part of daily life. We may as well make use of our linguistic knowledge to good effect.

For example, in a mixed-sex meeting we can support the right of other women speakers to be heard, even though we might not agree with them. We can encourage more hesitant women to enter the discussion, perhaps merely asking if they agree or disagree with a statement. We can develop the more co-operative aspects of our style, listening attentively and building on the points made by previous speakers.

It is important that we stop thinking of women's voices as unpleasant. Female voices are said to be shrill, shrieking, moaning, nagging, strident and so on. If you think about it, there are few such adjectives for male voices. It is true that women use four registers of pitch while men use three, but that does not mean higher-pitched voices sound unpleasant. We have merely been accustomed through the centuries to hear such descriptions of our voices. If we listen better we may find that as women have a greater range of pitch so they may develop a greater rhetorical and more interesting range when it comes to speaking.

Clearly some women (and men) in public life have chosen to alter the way they speak. Margaret Thatcher lowered the pitch of her voice by half the average difference in pitch between male and female voices. She apparently achieved this by humming exercises and a tutor from the National Theatre.

If you wish to lower your voice try speaking from the diaphragm not the throat. Remember to take a couple of relaxed breaths (no gulps) at the end of sections in any lengthy speech you might make so that your voice doesn't suddenly change up an octave. However, upon occasion you may have to raise your voice. Prime Minister's question time forced Mrs Thatcher to raise her pitch level just to be heard above the hubbub.

If you do decide to change your voice in certain respects, do practise your speaking or you might sound very artificial or monotonous. Our voices tend to vary in pitch according to the relative importance we give to the points we are making, at the beginnings and ends of sentences and with questions and commands. Some people believe women query more frequently than men do and there have been some suggestions that we place questions at the end of statements such as 'We'll go shopping this afternoon, *shall we?*' or 'They're an excellent buy, *don't you think?*' There seems *no* reliable evidence for this belief. So don't be put off by any comments you might see or hear concerning women's hesitancy and unnecessary questions.

Variation of pitch is much more attractive than a monotonous drone and there is some danger of the latter if you concentrate too much on a lower pitch. Sound affirmative and be in control. *You* decide how you want to talk and your increasing confidence will add assurance without stridency to your tone. And that's what we all want, after all.

WOMEN AND WRITING

Much research into children's language development indicates how closely the ability to write or decode the written word is tied in with speaking. Children proceed with writing and reading more competently if they speak fluently. As adults we should not disregard these interconnections. Writing can help our speaking and vice versa.

Women have written for centuries but usually in what is considered a private capacity. They wrote diaries not intended for publication and copious reams of letters. The writer, Dale Spender, claims that even novel-writing is a form of private writing, in that it is most often women writing mainly for women. We clearly have a need for expression, whatever the outlets for publication.

Diaries

Writing a diary, even a sporadic one, can prove helpful. It encourages reflection and scrutiny of any problems connected with managing your own life more effectively. The act of writing does concentrate the mind, even if you think the writing itself appears rambling. Virginia Woolf chose to write a diary even though she had plenty of other outlets for her writing, so that she could write in a looser, freer manner than when she wrote fiction or essays. It may be she also had a need for a private rather than public kind of writing, where she need not worry about audience and could deal with matters of importance to her which might not appear so for anyone else. She wrote in a book like an exercise book, not a diary with dates, so that there was no compulsion to write every day. You could keep a loose-leaf file and add pages (with dates) when you feel like writing.

Keeping an account of what happens to you, how you act and what your feelings are will be of interest in subsequent years. It also reveals certain patterns in the way you live. It might indicate an interest that could well be developed further, or it might reveal a pattern to feelings of depression which would indicate they were not casual moods brought about by isolated circumstances but something that needs talking over.

Exercises

Writing a diary has many benefits but it is something you decide to do yourself. Even if you decide to read parts of it out to others, diary-writing is hardly a group activity. Writing is, however, often collaborative, despite the romantic images of solitary poets wandering the moors or lonely novelists writing feverishly in garrets. There are a number of collections of short stories now that have been conceived and executed as a group activity. If you decide that you wish to write as a group (any number from three upwards) then you can choose to write in any style you wish about subjects that interest you. Or you can explore a series of exercises that encompass differing aims and encourage use of different styles and techniques. We include therefore a series of such exercises which we know have proved useful and enjoyable. Women have been surprised at how well they write and have enjoyed sharing their work with each other and the sense of achievement that a piece of writing brings. For many women writing had consisted for years of a few personal letters, lists and completing forms. This was the first occasion, perhaps since school, that they had considered writing at any length or for themselves. It is true that during the writing process they may well have rung each other up in great anxiety. A certain amount of self-doubt is quite in order but should not discourage completely.

Case study

Judith Walker heard about a New Opportunities for Women course from a local radio broadcast. She was 37 years old at the time, having had her career plans changed at just 18, when she had to leave the course she'd just started – Institutional Management – in order to care for and nurse her mother full-time. Later, when her mother's health improved, she married and enjoyed raising her two lively daughters. She never took up paid employment.

> I came on the course with an open mind, as I had no preconceived ideas about what to expect from it. I felt ready to learn and receive.
>
> The NOW course was an eye-opener for me and the start of new opportunities for me to perceive myself differently, in a more positive way, as my self-esteem and self-value and respect rose and I saw a 'new direction' in my life as new perceptions helped me change for the better. Things that I found extremely hard to do, as a teenager, like writing essays and reading aloud,

I found I could tackle, albeit with determination and perseverance, and felt a sense of achievement too.

I can see that NOW course as a changing-point in my life, as I shed 'roles' and became freer to be myself. The writing that started to flow on the course proved to be a means of unblocking the creative and previously suppressed sides of my nature, and the growth to becoming more whole as a person is currently my aim, as well as autonomy. Counselling courses have helped me in this goal.

Invisible writing

Like most invisibility this is more in the mind than reality. Many women do feel very hesitant about putting pen to paper, or finger to typewriter or word-processor, perhaps after a gap of some years. It may also be difficult if members of your family show surprise and even irritation at such activity, especially if they laugh at you. Apparently it is all right (or not too annoying) for mothers to sit and read, even if a little surprising. But when they start to write they look purposeful! One woman told us that as soon as she took up her pen it became a signal for a number of requests from her family – clean socks? calculator? food? where is the dictionary? Anything, just to interrupt. You will have to be quite firm about retaining your hour or whatever you need and *then* you can tell them where their socks are.

Having sorted out your family or partner or friends, you still have the problem of writing. The important thing is to start writing, without bothering about the spelling or the style. The invisibility comes from not showing what you have written to anyone unless you want to. We suggest you choose something which interests you, if you are writing for yourself, or else a subject which you have decided on as a group. It should be a fairly wide topic such as marriage or education, and then no one will be inhibited by its narrowness. It also makes the sharing of ideas much more interesting. In our experience only a very small number of women have kept their writing 'invisible' when it actually came to group discussion. Usually this was for very personal reasons. The writing referred to experiences the writer was not yet prepared to talk about openly. However, everyone valued the feeling of relief that they could write knowing they need not show it to anyone. Even if you keep it 'invisible', you've still got the piece and can refer to it at any time.

Focus

This exercise requires acknowledgement, accepting your own writing, even becoming quite proud of it. After the first piece of writing on a broad topic try to narrow the focus so that you are marshalling your ideas to a particular end. For instance, after writing and discussing the topic 'education' you may decide you are only interested in nursery education or adult literacy or returning to study courses or teaching history or student grants. You will find that your style of writing will probably change in subtle ways. It is worth looking at your first and second pieces to see in what ways they are different. This time you really should share the written piece with someone.

Work autobiography

This can prove to be one of the most useful exercises you complete. It can also cheer you up when you write about all the things you have done – and *don't* make that immediate comeback that you haven't done anything! Everyone has. Therefore everyone has had a variety of experiences and learnt a variety of skills either from those experiences or from learning how to deal with problems arising from them. This is where your uniqueness lies. Only you have had these series of experiences in this order. You are the best person to understand what strengths and abilities you've gained.

The work autobiography has to be detailed to be really useful and therefore you can't finish it in a side and a half. Some people say you need between thirty and fifty sides. That may sound very dispiriting, even to people who write quite often, so the best thing is to write in as much detail as you can and give yourself a week at least to do it in. You can write a few paragraphs each day. Remember to leave space, either by writing on alternate lines or by leaving gaps, or both. Items will come back into your mind after you've finished writing about one job or experience and you will need to go back and fill in the extra details. Refer back to the lifeline exercise if you did this as part of your self-assessment.

Start with your school life: which subjects did you take, which ones did you prefer, which ones were you good at? There may be a discrepancy between junior school and secondary. You may have been excellent at sums and then for some reason not realized your talent at Maths. Since many girls in the past dropped Maths far too early, it seems likely they were not encouraged. Did you belong to any clubs or societies? Did you keep up a fairly lengthy pen-friend correspondence? Did you write for a school magazine? Did you like physical activity (such as dancing) even if you didn't like sports? Or were you good at sports? Did you have responsibilities in the school or at home? Did you have part-time or weekend jobs? Did you have to get used to a number of different schools and communities because your parents moved frequently? In which case you probably developed skills to deal with new situations.

Then take each job and further training or college or university experience separately. Write down what you actually did. Often women have more responsibility than their job title appears to give them, so it's worth thinking back over what you did. Include times when you were looking after children or elderly or disabled dependants – all very valuable *work*. Include voluntary work and work experience such as being treasurer of a small (or large) group, perhaps of a charity, and responsibility for accounts or for organizing fund-raising events. You may have been on an interviewing panel (if so, this will be good experience for you to remember as an interviewee). Have you always been particularly good at house decoration? Have you had other educational or training experience along the way?

We can guarantee that you will be surprised at how much you *have* done. And there will be more to come.

However, don't write down value judgements such as 'I made a disaster of my first job' or 'the boss always picked on me and never gave me the chances others got' or 'it took me four years to get my degree and it should have taken three' – all of this may or may not be true, but we're interested in what you've *learnt* and *acquired*.

Skills search

Now that you've completed this mammoth task, go back over it! Read through all the detail and on a separate page indicate the skills you've acquired at each stage of your life. Some will recur. Look at the opportunities you took and those you didn't – if you have some regret about chances you didn't take, it may be time to do something about them now. Did you have responsibility for managing or organizing anything? Do you find it particularly easy to communicate with certain groups, e.g. with old people? What kinds of financial transactions have you been involved with?

We include a list of skills you may find helpful to consider. It is by no means exhaustive, so do add others.

administrating communicating co-ordinating delegating designing directing encouraging estimating evaluating examining guiding implementing improving innovating inspecting instructing interpreting performing persuading producing promoting reconciling renovating reporting researching teaching (this doesn't have to be in a classroom necessarily) training using your artistic talents

When you have done this, give it to someone else to read or preferably swap autobiographies if they've done the same exercise. Let them see if they can add a few more skills (and you to theirs). Another eye can often pin-point something you've missed.

Now you can begin to evaluate. What can you develop? What have you spent a surprising amount of time doing? What did you break off and might like to go back to? Where do your skills appear to be leading you? Does this agree with your preferences?

You can tie in this material with the answers you came up with doing the personal assessment exercises in Chapter One.

A helpful addition to the skill selection exercise

Look *again* through your work autobiography and note down the number of times you've exploited a particular skill and the different situations in which you've used it. For example, organizational or financial skills may have been apparent at several different stages of your life, in your first job or your second job, as part of a voluntary group, as a mother. List the six or seven skills most frequently used, since they are the substance of what you have to offer as a prospective employee, student or voluntary worker. Write about one or two pages on *each* of these skills, including the actual situations and length of time involved. Give yourself credit for any connected achievements, even if no one else did at the time. Good, conscientious work can unfortunately be overlooked. Then order in importance the six or seven skills on the basis of (a) those in which you are most competent and (b) which ones you most enjoy performing. You now have the basic material for giving yourself confidence in your abilities and achievements to be considered in any interview.

Self-discovery

We can also use our writing as a form of exploration, of self-discovery, which enables us to understand our own system of values. We are not always entirely clear about the values we hold but when they have surfaced quite definitely in our writing they can be an important element in the decisions we make.

Write a short character study of yourself, perhaps in the third person. Discuss your philosophy of life, any views you have on business, social and public affairs, law, your own goals and anything else you consider relevant. We include one such study by **Esmé Talbot**. You can see that her attitudes would indicate specific career choices.

Basically you make an effort for yourself; no one else will do it for you. There is a price for every decision you make, which means there are very few right or wrong decisions. There is always a choice, however desperate or negative a situation appears at the time. Even if you're aware of the options you may not wish to take them because you realize you couldn't live with the pay-off in the medium or long term. As long as you are mentally and physically fit you have a responsibility to try to be self-reliant.

Business is a terrific way of tapping energy and I think money is a great motivation for action but the problem comes with greed. Where people wouldn't dream of cutting corners in private life they will in business. But philosophies such as corporate responsibility either in business or in the National Health Service or the Town Hall are ineffective. Managers then duck taking hard or unpopular decisions, particularly in a group or committee.

I like the energy, the guts, the initiative people show

in business, it's risky and scary. A lot of women have hobby enterprises, it's an occupation rather than playing it up at the sharp end.

Social stability is enormously important for the stability of a society. Shops and pubs are necessary as places people can go to for a neutral reason. Employment is competitive. Though people show some small change in sociability they are looking for large gains, opportunities to edge their way up. Even with the smallest modicum of ambition you learn to guard yourself. Public life means you attempt to balance the rights you want from society with your responsibilities towards it. There has to be a balance. I'm much more law-abiding now than I was as a teenager. I feel comfortable being honest but will lie to be tactful.

A family can have two careers, not three. The children are one career. I'm torn not utilizing my qualifications gained before the children came. I've ended up in the same position as those who didn't try. Nevertheless my daughters are my fundamental responsibility, I cannot delegate that to paid help. I should like to do more work from home, more as a JP. I would like a chunk that was something of my own – lecturing or a business. Not working in a chartered accountants', the last bastion of male conservatism. I couldn't become a partner. You're only as good as your next job. So I'd like something independent. Perhaps a tax adviser. I don't want to be an unreliable female, so I want a specialist area in a small field.

Such an exercise may help you decide where you want to go, or to look for a particular employment situation, for instance a small unit attached to a large organization rather than a job in the large organization itself. You may find you prefer a hierarchical establishment, particularly one that offers quick promotion for certain talents. Or you may decide to be as independent as possible and run your own business.

Exploration of values

Another 'value' exercise which makes you stop and think 'Perhaps I should organize my life differently' is to write down the answers to two questions. This exercise will require some thought but probably take up only one side of a sheet of paper.

1 What major achievements would I like to see occur during my lifetime?
2 What world or country problems would I like to see solved? Can I help with either?

The nature of such questions tends to encourage broad answers and you may think contributing to any solution is beyond your reach. Consider some possible answers. For instance, one response to the first question might be 'Reduce world starvation' or something like that. A response to the second might be 'Save the rain forests'. You feel your individual contribution isn't going to change anything but consider what you might do. You could join any one of a number of organizations helping in this area or make a particular effort to buy goods from the Third World. Think of practical applications. Have you done anything to save trees in your own environment or encouraged other people to grow some or grown some yourself?

At any rate you probably wouldn't want to work for a business which was completely in conflict with what you would like to see achieved. Discussing your answers with another person or as part of a group will help you clarify how important such issues are to you. As Esmé Talbot pointed out, our values change according to our age, our circumstances and our knowledge. You may feel like altering your life-style a little to accomplish rather more in the directions *you* find important.

Colleagues

Think of the kinds of people you tend to like and dislike. Write down (and perhaps discuss afterwards) sketches of between eight and ten types in total. You may like more than you dislike or vice versa; you don't have to have even numbers! Although these sketches may be based on people you know, don't give them names, since you're considering types rather than individuals. This exercise encourages you to think about potential colleagues.

What kinds of people would you most like to work with? How do you see yourself fitting into a team? What do you have to offer in terms of getting on with people? Are there some kinds of behaviour you would find intolerable?

Although we can choose our friends and to some extent the relations with whom we wish to remain in contact, it is true we cannot select working colleagues in the same manner. The whole area of behaviour and relationships at work is an extremely significant part of our working environment. It is therefore very useful to realize our own limitations, priorities and capabilities in this direction.

Now you have completed some or all of these exercises you can probably think of other value areas you'd like to write about and/or discuss, to clarify your own mind. All such exercises help you to consider what you want from your life and work and what you can contribute. Just because there is a great deal of hype at the moment about women returners doesn't mean you have to take the first job that appears.

Ideal advertisement

Write an advertisement you would like to see in a newspaper or job agency that you could apply for. To do this you will need to look at a selection of advertisements first. Here is a selection of words and phrases from current advertisements:

innovation free-thinking problem-solvers good communication analytical skills naturally enthusiastic self-motivated willing to learn determination work in a team capacity vital member of a new team high degree of responsibility initiative bright and energetic experienced creative thorough, practical knowledge proven ability training provided if necessary previous experience not essential foreign languages useful no-smoking offices ability to work without supervision personality and confidence job satisfaction interesting travel competitive salary structure versatile second-jobbers for responsible positions logical and common-sense approach ideally one year's experience highly efficient excellent organizational skills suit a self-starter eye for detail astute pension scheme communicate clearly and persuasively flair for design sound judgement salary negotiable self-reliant hard-working fit dynamic lively self-motivated demanding post relocation assistance competent work to deadlines exciting excellent promotion prospects

Note that they occasionally describe the environment (non-smoking rooms) and offer inducements (car, pension, training, promotion prospects). Some require previous experience, others do not. Note also the adjectives used to describe the job they're offering and their view of the ideal candidate. Fashions change in advertisements just the same as everywhere else and you may well find a different crop of words in three years' time.

Make a selection of these phrases that are appropriate for you. Are you determined, logical, dynamic, self-motivated or . . .? Do you have experience or need it?

When you have written the ideal advertisement for you to answer, write your ideal job specification. This is not the same exercise, if you think about it. The ideal advertisement makes you consider the requirements of employers, the choice between small and large organizations, the qualities they want in an employee – even though it's ideally suited to you. The ideal job *specification* concerns what you want in terms of hours, conditions of employment, actual promotion prospects (what you want to be doing in five years), degree of responsibility, the job in which you could be happiest and most productive.

We're all realistic enough to know that ideal advertisements and jobs are few and far between but both these exercises will give you markers as to what you're looking for.

Writing and therapy

We have been considering how writing focuses our thoughts but it can release as well as concentrate. Writing does have a therapeutic side. It is possible to use your own writing to bring tensions and problems to the surface. You can 'write out' painful parts of your own history, scenes that you cannot readily discuss with other people. You can rewrite such scenes giving yourself words you never used at the time. Probably you couldn't answer back effectively at the time anyway. Now you can. Also you can write an imaginary conversation with a colleague at work or at home in which you express all your anger and frustration at some matter which is annoying you. There is a real satisfaction in writing such a one-sided dialogue, screwing it up into a crumpled-ball and throwing it with all your force into a waste-paper basket, the rubbish-bin or the fire. You won't have got rid of the situation which is causing your anger but you have released some of your emotions about it in a very beneficial way.

Similarly you can write when you're depressed and even perhaps see some kind of pattern in depression. People are not really ignoring or neglecting you, it's what you think now perhaps, and if you look at your writing you can see that's what you thought three months ago as well. It then becomes a feature of depression, not a sign that other people have negative responses to you. Writing for such reasons can be accomplished in a group or by yourself, depending on how you feel about what you're expressing. Some material you may want to keep to yourself.

One thousand-word project

Writing one thousand words seems daunting to many people. If you do decide to undertake such a project, however, you will feel extremely satisfied when you have completed it and will realize you could do it again much more easily and that you probably needed more than one thousand words in the first place.

Many women returners have found this a very rewarding exercise, to judge by their comments. They found it helpful to have several short discussion sessions about selecting topics, encouraging each other and commenting on their progress (or lack of it). The topic could be anything which you feel you could write on at some length. It could deal with events in the past or with future plans or be connected with some area of interest to *you*. Some subjects previously chosen include: the history of an old house now demolished in which grandparents lived, early childhood memories, the history of knitting, planning the decoration and furnishing of a larger, older house than the one currently lived in, the importance of position in families (for instance, whether you were first-born, youngest of six, etc.), memories of several years in Spain (written for a daughter who was born and spent her early years there). Some students chose to research areas which would help them in interviews for jobs or courses or setting up businesses: for example, spending time in a careers adviser's office (or any other employment) and writing about that, researching wallpaper designs, the education of Henry VIII, environmental issues. Some have written on personal issues which they wanted to come to terms with, for example a divorce or unhappy childhood.

If you are working with a group choose a date for completion so that you have a deadline to meet. That is an effective learning discipline in itself. Then select a time when you can display and discuss your work. Some will have graphs or pictures to show. Either a tutor or you can select two or three paragraphs to read out to the group. You may not wish to share very personal material with a larger group but keep to the deadline and the work length.

Such a display and discussion session proves how much we learn from each other and how enjoyable learning can be. It can often be the climax to a particular section of a course or series of group meetings.

Visibility and audibility

In the final section to this chapter we would like you to consider your future goals in terms of being seen and heard. Women are not very visible in public life – partly because we are so visible in advertisements and TV stereotypes as a particular kind of person, ranging from page-three 'luscious beauties' to women 'selling' cars or drainage pipes (as in trade catalogues) or, in a rather different manner, detergents and cosmetics. We must use our abilities and talents in communication to present our ideas and range of achievements more effectively. This means examining the connections between language, status, power relations and discrimination. We need more women to write about their experiences at work, to make known their feelings about the whole range of discrimination experience – from sexual harassment to being excluded from business conversations in pubs, or not getting the promotion at the right time. We also need to concern ourselves more with speaking, so that we feel more empowered to use our undeniable talents in this field. Words, whether in talking or writing, are extremely important in furthering our individual aims and making for a society in which we can see 50 per cent of the people in the news being women, negotiating trade agreements and new laws as well as their present role as 'human interest' stories.

If you wish to read further on language matters, consult the Reading List at the end of the book.

4

FINDING WORK

This chapter covers job hunting – where to look for jobs, how to apply, some tips on how to present yourself at an interview, job-sharing and flexible work – and it also looks at the question of self-employment or working in partnership with others. First of all, though, there is a brief overview of the employment scene in general to give you a broader picture of what the 1990s could mean for women.

The labour market

By the late 1980s, it had become increasingly obvious that the drop in the birth-rates which occurred in the 1960s and 1970s was beginning to have an effect on Britain's employment patterns. Demographic statistics show the number of 16- to 19-year-olds in the population falling sharply and, as a result, the pool of school-leavers available for work also shrinking. A drop of 37 per cent in the numbers of school-leavers and young people going into work has been estimated. This trend is likely to continue in the 1990s before falling off towards the latter part of the decade. The numbers of people entering the work-force are going to be further reduced by the increasing proportion of young people expected to stay in education after 16 years old.

The shortfall creates serious problems, long- and short-term, for many employers. There will, for example, be fierce competition in industry and commerce to recruit available school-leavers, students with higher qualifications and people from a broader labour market than in the past. This is good news for women who want paid employment or a career because employers need to recruit and train adults who want to return to the labour market in order to make up the shortfall. A similar situation occurred during the Second World War, when there was a concerted effort to recruit women for work outside the home because so many men had been called up to fight in the war. The experience, abilities and enthusiasm of mature women are valued today as almost never before. And it should be a good time to capitalize on the spirit as well as the letter of equal opportunities.

Employers are increasingly looking to women returners (as well as older workers and other previously disadvantaged groups generally) and the more enlightened ones are offering attractive inducements such as work-place nurseries, career break schemes, interesting part-time work or flexible working arrangements to attract or retain people with other responsibilities. In some regions, at least, the labour market has become a seller's market and those companies who could be described as 'caring', who provide good working conditions and support services like stress counsellors, are the ones that are more likely to attract and keep their work-force.

Another factor which encourages people back to paid work is training. It should make economic sense to an employer to offer training with a job. It keeps the work-force up to date and they are more likely to stay because of the provision of ongoing off-the-job and on-the-job training. If you apply for a job and get an interview, bear this in mind. Ask if training goes with the job and show how interested you would be if it did.

More and more employers, especially in smaller businesses, are realizing that training is part and parcel of a business – an investment, not a cost. It is essential if employers want to respond to demographic changes and meet future skill needs. It also makes for a more motivated and committed work-force.

Various reports have shown that Britain has lagged behind some other industrialized countries in its provision of training, and women in particular have generally fared less well than men in getting the training they need. Research shows that women gain considerable benefit from training and that for many it is a major turning-point in their lives.

The problem facing British industry in the 1990s is not just one of staff shortages. There are indications that there is a decline in the number of lower-level jobs and an increase in jobs at a higher level. It is vital for women to get a slice of the action and become involved in training that is designed to bring their skills up to date or to train them to a higher level.

Too often people become pigeon-holed at work. Their appearance, their original qualifications or their sex can make it difficult for employers to imagine them in different work environments. Not only does this attitude harm individual career prospects but it can also lead to companies overlooking the mass of untapped talent already on the payroll. Some women are employed in work where they are unable to use their talents and intelligence. Others may feel that they are contributing far more in terms of management or administrative input than is being recognized and would therefore welcome the chance of proving their skills in a new situation. Not everyone will or wants to achieve a total job change. But a greater awareness of the pay-offs of developing people at work through, for example, redeployment is another of the side-effects of demographic, economic and social changes in Britain.

In the longer term other factors affecting employment trends which will be of particular interest to women may come into play. Changes in the whole concept of work, patterns of work and leisure and the further impact of technologies are some examples. Obviously these questions are beyond the scope of this book but they are particularly relevant to women because in general they are probably more flexible in their approach and attitudes to work and may benefit from an era where there will be less traditional employment patterns.

Preparation and planning

Time spent on preparing yourself for going back to work, thinking about what you want or need and building up your personal profile and experience and your confidence, is time well spent. Some women may rush back to work because they feel they are not making a financial contribution to the household. It's always better to do some homework first.

Try not to feel guilty or pressured into getting the first job that comes along. This can often undermine the desire and capacity to take a longer-term view. For example, women will often take short courses which will get them a job quickly but which may not lead to a fulfilling career. They may decide not to train for professional work because of the length of time it takes to get a qualification and the consequent feelings of guilt at being a 'drain' on family resources.

The material in Chapter One and writing your own work autobiography in Chapter Three will have given you some ideas and tools which you can use when it comes to getting to know yourself and consequently the kind of job you want. We hope that by the time you are reading this you are clearer about your capabilities, ambitions, values, personality and interests. You also need to think about how much money you need to or want to earn. You must weigh up the consequences of your returning to work, whether indeed it is for you, whether the stress and upheaval are worth it, whether some other form of activity outside the home would be better in the short term.

If you need to clarify your next step, do this refresher exercise. Make a list of what you like to do, what you don't like doing, what you can do and what you can't. Don't underestimate your experience as a housewife if that is what you have been for the past few years. Your potential value to an employer has probably been enhanced by some of the things you have been doing even though they have been unpaid.

Don't forget you have probably been a financial manager, personnel manager, child-care expert, cook, interior decorator and so on whilst you have been 'just a housewife and mother'. These are valuable skills and marketable assets.

Drawing up a list of what you enjoy doing, your hobbies and interests and your skills as a mother and/or housewife will probably reveal talents and abilities you hadn't realized you had and may mean you don't go back to the kind of work you dislike. It will help you get a clearer picture of the sort of work you might look for. For instance if you like figure work, it's worth looking for a job such as a cashier. In order to prepare for this kind of work you might think of volunteering to be treasurer of any club or society you belong to. If you feel a bit stale and need updating you could enrol for a 'Brush Up Your Maths' or similar refresher or access-type courses. You may, however, want to move straight on to a more advanced course such as a GCSE or A Level at a local tertiary college if you think you're up to it. (See Chapter Five for advice on training and education.)

Careers guidance

Setting out on a new career isn't always easy – new jobs and professions are emerging as a result of changes in technology and the emergence of new industries. You can't expect to keep up with all the latest developments. Talk to friends and family about job prospects; they may have a different and useful perspective or, better still, contacts. If you're still not sure what you want to do, you can of course seek professional career guidance.

Career consultants will advise you on your future prospects. Using in-depth interview techniques or questionnaires, a professional career analyst can uncover aspects of yourself and your aptitudes and suitability for certain kinds of work or training, pin-point strengths and weaknesses and suggest specific career paths. Many will help with writing your curriculum vitae (c.v.). There are a number of careers advisory services that specialize in guidance and counselling for women (see the address list at the end of the book). This service will cost money and you need to find out how much before you take this route.

All large towns and cities will have a *Careers Service* run by the Local Authority and many offer adult guidance services. You can make an appointment with an adult careers officer and use other services they offer such as a job-share register or seminars and talks on careers. The Careers Office will have up-to-date information on jobs, training, polytechnic and university courses nationally and locally and local tertiary college provision. Virtually all Careers Offices have a library where you can browse through careers literature, prospectuses, brochures and booklets as well as watch videos or use their computerized data banks. Careers officers are professionally trained and can offer independent, unbiased and free advice. They know about your local employment situation and are in touch with employers, colleges, training schemes and so on.

Jobcentres in most towns and cities, are also good sources of information. They are staffed by people who know about the local and national job picture and display vacancies on their premises. Jobcentres also give information on training courses and special schemes that might help and also about job-hunting methods. You may find that at the Jobcentre you are routed into work that is thought appropriate to women. In other words there are still traditional assumptions about what is women's work and what is men's work. If you want to work in a non-traditional occupation such as engineering or electronics, stick out for these kinds of jobs and don't be put off by entrenched attitudes based on stereotypes.

Jobclubs run by Jobcentres are particularly successful at helping women find jobs – in fact the success rate for women is around 3 per cent higher than for men. If you have been out of work for six months or more you can join a Jobclub. Women who have been away from work because of family responsibilities are eligible to join even though they are unlikely to be registered unemployed. The aim is to help you make a success of job-hunting – giving you advice on job-hunting techniques, preparing a c.v., practice for interviews and filling in application forms. They provide stamps, stationery, newspapers and directories, as well as telephones, photocopiers and typewriters, and give you a place to work so that you can make the most of these facilities.

There are plenty of people or organizations around to give advice. It is almost a full-time job tracking them down and sifting through all the information. Try not to be put off by negative comments about your age or lack of experience. When you go for a job you are likely to find yourself in competition with many other people, some of them younger, seemingly fresher, brighter and more recently qualified. It can be easy to lose heart and feel rejected before you start. Never give up, however hopeless it seems: there is always something you can do.

Be positive and be organized – keep a diary or use an exercise book to keep track of the enquiries you have made, the advice you have received, the appointments you have had and the jobs you apply for. Keep copies of any job advertisements, letters or application forms, a schedule of the interviews you go for and if possible your own post-mortem of the interview itself. This kind of discipline is in itself good practice for your working life later on.

If you are determined about getting a job, treat job-hunting as a job. Get up in the morning with a plan for the day. If you were working in an office this would be called 'time management'. It is a very useful procedure and you might as well get some practice at it. If possible, dress as if you were going to work or at least don't put on your sloppiest clothes. Take yourself and your job-hunting seriously. It will give you more confidence if you feel you look good. Too many women are half-hearted about careers and don't have enough self-worth when it comes to the contribution they make in the work-place. You have a right to a job if that is what you want. Women will not have good careers until they take their working lives seriously. This means, as we said in the Introduction, not drifting along in the hope that something will turn up. It won't unless you make it.

Get organized. This may sound a bit unrealistic if you are running a home and looking after children or relatives at the same time. But it might pay off to arrange care for these dependants during some part of the day whilst you are looking around in order to give everyone a taste of what the future might hold. Friends, relatives, partners and women like you will all help out if there is a dearth of other facilities in your area. After all you'd do the same for them.

Where to look for a job

A lot of job-seeking is common sense. If you are looking for work you could mention it to friends and colleagues; they probably have friends, partners or networks of contacts that could prove useful. Look in the 'Situations Vacant' column of the local newspaper. Get into the habit of reading it regularly and try to see the paper as soon as it comes out. You might try reading the business pages of local papers because they give you an idea about job prospects generally – which firms are closing down or which opening up in your locality. If you notice that a company is moving to your area or a new one starting up, you could try the *speculative* approach.

The 'spec' approach means getting in touch with a firm, even if they are not advertising any vacancies, either by phone, by letter or by calling in. Lots of jobs are not advertised. People get them through friends or relatives passing the word around. If you decide to send a letter on spec, write confidently but politely, stating you'd like the chance to get started and would appreciate advice and information. You should say why you are writing, what relevant experience you have, when you're available for interview and when you could start work, and enclose a copy of your c.v. Remember to keep a copy of the letter. Don't expect

23 Chapeltown Road
Sheffield S16

Tel.: 0742–772396

Mrs. A. Pettit
Personnel Manager
Tresses
High Street
Meadowhall
Sheffield

Dear Mrs Pettit

I saw in today's *Star* that you will shortly be opening a new salon at the Meadowhall Shopping Centre and I would like to work with you.

I served a three-year apprenticeship as a hairdresser with Salon One and during that time, through part-time study, gained the City and Guilds 760 certificate in Ladies' and Men's Hairdressing. I then worked with Hair Associates Ltd for three years until leaving to bring up my children seven years ago. These were both town centre salons and I gained a wide experience of cutting both men's and women's hair, also bleaching, tinting, and perming in the latest styles.

I am 29 years old and I am available for full-time work and prepared to work on Saturdays and late evenings as required.

I am available for interview any time and could start work immediately if required. I can provide references from my two previous employers.

I look forward to hearing from you.

Yours sincerely

Ann Green

miracles but don't give up – it may be months before someone replies because a suitable position might not be available at the time of your writing but may come up later. You could follow up your initial letter either in writing or by phone. People who are blessed with firm but gentle and polite persistence seldom stay unemployed for long. Everyone is impressed by determination and guts and for some jobs, these might count more than academic qualifications.

We have mentioned Jobcentres as a source of information on job vacancies and there are also *private employment agencies*. They serve the needs of employers and employees, and most offer a personal job-finding interview to help you get to grips with the situation. You will find a list of agencies in the Yellow Pages.

The 'first impression' rule

It is sometimes said that if you want to make a good impression on someone, you have approximately thirty seconds in which to do it. That is the length of time that it takes for us to absorb vital information about a person which we use as a guide for all further encounters. We'll deal with this later when we discuss interviews but the same principle applies to other aspects of selling yourself to a potential employer.

You have probably clarified your ambitions and skills and what you have to offer through the self-analysis suggested in this and previous chapters. This can be used as the foundation for writing a curriculum vitae. This is often the vital first step towards finding a job. A well-prepared, well-laid-out c.v. can make a good first impression.

You may not always need to send a c.v. if you are applying for a job because the organization may ask you to fill in an application form. But you will need one prepared if you are writing on the off-chance that a company has a suitable vacancy. You will also need one if you are applying for grants or loans for either educational or business purposes. You may find that preparing one will improve your self-esteem by forcing you to focus on your qualifications and achievements.

The curriculum vitae

A curriculum vitae (c.v.) is a record of yourself, your job experience, schooling and any qualifications or interests, listed as briefly as possible. Always be honest while giving the best possible impression of yourself when writing a c.v. Don't say you can speak French if you can't; don't put down any examinations that you have failed. If you have failed any just don't mention them. Avoid trying to be witty – it doesn't usually go down well.

Some golden rules:

1 Type out your c.v. on plain A4 paper. Don't use coloured paper unless you are sure that this is appropriate for the firm you are applying to. If you can't type, ask someone who can to help you.
2 Once you have it typed out, check the c.v. for errors, omissions, etc. Spelling mistakes can look bad.
3 Keep it short and to the point – one or two pages at most. Don't bore a potential employer with reams of your life history.
4 Include all *essential* information, starting with the present and working backwards in time. Begin with your most recent job (give dates), your school career (with dates), exams passed. Include a section on special skills (e.g. a driving licence), interests, any positions of responsibility you might hold.
5 You can include references here. Ideally these should be people who know you and who have some authority or standing; for example, a former teacher, a bank manager, a former employer, the headteacher of your child's school if you are an active parent.

   Finding someone to put in a good word for you is not always easy if you've been out of things for a bit. That is why, if you are planning to return to work, you should get 'plugged in' to things in advance. Joining any kind of course, particularly an access or women returner's course, would provide you with a suitable referee.

You may find it difficult writing out a c.v. if your exams and work experience date from some years back. Even so, it's worth mentioning them. Present what experience you have in a brief, positive and matter-of-fact way. Include up-to-date and relevant activities, not forgetting the skills developed at home or doing voluntary work, and highlight their value for the job for which

CURRICULUM VITAE

PERSONAL DETAILS
Name   Zita Pratesh
Address   1 Villa Road   Bristol BR2 1PR
Telephone   0272-764228
Date of Birth 6 May 1960
Nationality   British
                  Married – a daughter and two sons

EDUCATION
I was educated up to the age of 15 in Cardiff.

1975–1978   St Margaret's School   Bristol
1978–1981   London University

QUALIFICATIONS

1976 O Levels   Eight including English and Maths
1978 A Levels   English (A), Geography (C)
1981   BA (Hons.) degree (2:2) English Language and Literature
1989   Qualified as Teacher of English as a Foreign Language

Clean driving licence since 1981
Life-saving certificate, swimming certificates

WORK EXPERIENCE*

1981–1983   Research Assistant at Edinburgh University engaged in project looking at second language and adult education. Visited many community education centres, evening institutes and the like. Left this post when I married and moved to the south.
1986–1989   Numerous part-time posts teaching English as a second language, English literature at adult education classes and WEA.

78

INTERESTS AND ACTIVITIES

Although I have not worked full-time since 1983, I have developed my interest in teaching adults and by taking English as a foreign language and English as a second language qualifications. I have done voluntary work with the Adult Literacy Scheme and with women whose first language is not English and who for cultural reasons remain largely housebound.

I have maintained my interest in swimming by teaching Mothers and Babies classes in the local swimming-baths.

I speak Urdu.

*Normally you should list your most recent job first and list all other jobs in reverse chronological order. In this case, Zita has only had one full-time job and she wishes to highlight it by putting it first, before the part-time work details.

CURRICULUM VITAE

Name   Sonia Williams
Address   23 Jubilee Road, Hackney, London
Tel   (071) 253 9811
Date of Birth   5.1.63

Education and Training GCSE Home Economics, Maths. Started hairdressing YTS. I have recently gone back to night school to do GCSE Sociology.

Employment Have worked in hairdressing salons, Chelsea Girl, cleaning, nursing auxiliary and nursery assistant.

Special Skills and Interests I like working with people and help at our church's youth club. I want to go further either in youth work or nursery nursing.

References Rev. Edward Linklater, Main Road Baptist Church, Hackney, Tel. (071) 397 2842. John Kelly, Youth Worker, Baptist Community Centre, Tel. (071) 393 4829.

you are now applying. If you have done any public speaking, such as in a PTA or at an environmental group, or are involved in local polititcs, this should be included in your c.v., as should involvement in Citizens' Advice Bureaux, Meals-on-Wheels, and so on. Don't dismiss hobbies or voluntary work done to a high standard – they create a good impression as long as you don't overdo it and come across as an evening-class or charity groupie.

Photocopy a dozen or so of these c.v.'s for future use. Employers will not mind receiving a copy but do not photocopy letters of application or covering letters. These must always be individually written to a human being rather than a title like 'The Managing Director' or 'The Personnel Manager'. Try to find out the name of these people by simply phoning up the firm and asking for their names.

You will find two sample c.v.'s on pp. 78 to 79, which will give you an idea of the general layout to follow.

Interviews

If you need advice on how to cope with an interview for a job you will find books devoted to the subject in your local library or Careers Office. However, here are a few basic dos and don'ts:

- **Be prepared** Find out as much as you can about the organization you may be joining, its size, what it does, etc., and find out about the job you might be doing.
- **What you might be asked** Think about what sort of questions might come up at the interview; why you would like the job, why you would be the best person for the job, your strengths and weaknesses. This is not easy, but try to make your weaknesses look like strengths and show how you have learnt from any mistakes.
- **Questions for the interviewer** Have a couple of questions (but not too many) for your interviewers. There may have been something not covered by the description of the job or you might want to ask about the opportunities for training.

Arrive for the interview early but not so early that you have too much spare time to make you anxious. If you do arrive too early, take the opportunity to find out more about the company. Don't worry about being nervous, the interviewer probably is too! Take a few deep breaths before you go into the interview room. We recommend that you don't shake hands with the interviewer (unless she offers a hand first). In Britain, it might be taken as being ingratiating or over-familiar. (In Europe handshaking is much more commonplace and would be expected.) Listen carefully to the questions. Talk clearly and try not to over-answer questions by talking too much. Look at the person interviewing you without staring hypnotically; this gives an impression of confidence and calm self-assurance.

It is said that the first five minutes of an interview are the most important. So concentrate your mind and expend your energy on this portion. A lot of decisions are made about you at the start and will determine whether there is sufficient interest in keeping you in the frame for the job. If you can't answer a question, say so or ask for clarification. If you feel flustered or nervous, take some good deep breaths. This should calm you down.

The way you dress for an interview is obviously important. You may feel that how you dress is an integral part of your personality and that it is none of an employer's business what you choose to wear. Unfortunately this attitude is a bit unrealistic and rightly or wrongly people are judged by their outward appearance – and women more so than men. Most people cannot afford to be too individualistic in their dress; save that for home.

Your image sends out lots of messages about yourself and is therefore important. If you dress too casually, it could mean you don't take yourself or the job you are applying for seriously. If you dress too flamboyantly it might be interpreted as being more interested in clothes than in the job.

If you are really worried about what to wear for an interview you might try to look around at what other women wear in that organization and in this way get a feel of what is expected. A good rule of thumb is to look fashionable rather than boring but tone down the extremes. One careers officer we consulted advised interviewees not to wear too much large costume jewellery. Think about your hair-style. A few pounds invested in a new hair-style from a good stylist may well be worth it, making you feel more relaxed and confident. We would advise against spending a fortune on new clothes and new hair-styles until you are established in a job. People dress quite casually for work these days so save your money until you've got more of an idea of what will fit in.

Posture and bearing are important too – someone who stands up straight and has a ready smile will always put herself at the front of the queue for a job. However, try not to smile so much that you don't come across as a serious candidate. Voice is also important. It is quite a personal matter and what is an attractive voice to some may grate on others. If you have a good speaking voice people usually think you are 'somebody', and, in these days of telephone communication, it is more important than ever. You don't necessarily have to invest in elocution lessons or lose a perfectly attractive regional accent and acquire BBC English, but try to speak clearly and grammatically. If possible ask a friend to give you a mock interview – rehearse your body language as well as your verbal answers.

If you fluff a question at an interview, take a deep breath and concentrate your thoughts on the next one. It's more than likely that you will be able to retrieve the situation.

Even in these days of equal opportunities legislation you may be asked questions that would not be asked of a man. For instance, an interviewer might ask what you would do if your

children were ill, or if you would be prepared to move around the country for the company, or how you would like working with much younger men who would be your managers. There is no easy answer as to how to react to these. Probably the best thing to do is to get round the question as tactfully as you can but there is no point in alienating the interviewer. As the old saying goes, 'More flies are caught by honey than by vinegar'. Remain polite even if you think questions are unfair. If you are rejected for a job try not to feel too miserable or angry. Take a positive view and try to capitalize on the experience.

You can learn a lot from interviews by trying to analyse your performance. You can gain confidence by taking notes on the kind of questions you were asked so that with more foresight you can do better next time. One writer, Liz Hodgkinson, gives this piece of advice in her book *Working Woman's Guide* (1985):

> If, after the interview, you hear that you have not landed the job, it is quite in order to write to the firm, thanking them for seeing you, and saying that you would still be interested in a job with them, should another suitable vacancy arise. This helps to lodge you more firmly in their minds, and stops them forgetting all about you.

Case studies

Bernice O'Mara:

I was very very nervous when I went for the interview. I had seen the job advertised in the paper and had phoned up the company. It was for a secretary to the sales manager. That was nerve-racking in itself. I didn't know what to say on the phone and ended up talking to the wrong person because I just didn't make myself clear. Eventually I got through to someone, who put me through to the sales manager, who asked some questions and then asked if I'd go and see him.

The actual interview was a bit of a blur. There were two of them – the office manageress and the sales manager. They asked me about myself, what I had been doing and the reasons why I wanted the job and why I thought I was the best person for it. That threw me. I hadn't expected that question. I think I mumbled something about the fact that I hadn't had much recent experience and had never used a word-processor but that I did, have typing qualifications and, well, just wanted something to get me out of the house now the kids were at school.

I realize now that I must have sounded very 'take it or leave it'. I hadn't realized that I needed to sound a bit more enthusiastic about the job, to 'sell' myself a bit better. I didn't think they would be interested in the things I did, like keep-fit or helping my brother-in-law out when he needed an extra pair of hands. I should have said that I was willing to learn how to use modern office equipment and would go to night school if necessary.

They did ask me about the children, what I would do if they were ill. I said I'd work something out but that they were never ill anyway. Looking back on it I think I talked too much. I just gabbled on. Next time I think I'd practise some answers and time myself.

I didn't get the job but I didn't want it anyway. The firm was very small. The only other woman there worked part-time and the sales manager was out a lot so there wouldn't have been anyone to talk to so I wouldn't have been any better off than at home. I suppose that's one good thing that came out of that first interview – sizing up the actual firm and seeing if it was the kind of place I wanted to work in. When I go for another interview I think I'll try to be better prepared and get my good points across.

Marilyn Hale is a Chief Administrative Officer with a city council. She has had a successful career in local government. She thinks that too many people take a very narrow view of their potential and don't see the benefits of change and broadening their experience. Here she talks about the advantages of taking risks *and* good preparation.

The first major hurdle in my career came when an administrative officer post became available in the Council's Highways Department. I was really interested in this but thought I didn't stand a chance of getting it because it would have been a big jump from a clerical to a semi-professional administration post. It was two grades above me and would also have meant a big increase in salary.

I got a lot of encouragement from my husband; who helped me overcome some of my doubts. I decided to apply for the job but realized that, if I was to have any chance, my application would have to be out of the ordinary and make an impact. Unless I did a superb application I was going to fail at the first hurdle; a lot of people don't realize this. When I wrote the application, I made the most of my experience; I put myself over as enthusiastic and committed and said that I was convinced I could do the job given the opportunity.

I was ecstatic when I was invited for interview but also terrified at the prospect. I then set about preparing for the interview. I found out more about the department and had a 'brainstorming' session with my husband about the kind of questions I would be asked. The interview went well and I felt less nervous because of the amount of preparation I had done. I was called back for a second, more gruelling interview with the Director of the Department and his Deputy because they had found me 'impressive' despite my lack of experience.

I have received a lot of support and encouragement in my various job moves so, if someone comes to me asking for advice about a job, I always sit down and help them with the application or help them prepare for an interview. I tell them to be positive, to stress their qualities and, where they lack experience, to show how their other qualities will compensate and how they've learned from experiences, even negative ones, which has allowed them to develop as a person.

DIFFERENT WAYS TO WORK

If you have been out of the job market for a while you might want to ease your way into it gradually or you may have many other interests and responsibilities that you want to keep going as well as doing paid work. The answer may be more flexible working arrangements such as working from home, free-lancing, part-time work or job-sharing. You might even consider setting up your own business.

Working from home

You may choose this option because it would seem to dovetail fairly easily into child-rearing and other domestic duties. If your career to date would allow you to work on a free-lance basis, all well and good. But free-lance work sometimes comes in fits and starts and you need to be prepared, say, to arrange for someone to look after children at short notice. We would defy anyone to be able to concentrate for very long with a demanding toddler around. Jobs that can be successfully carried out at home include: typing, secretarial services and translation work, indexing, proof-reading and most kinds of art or craft work. Of course, if you were a dental technician or a physics teacher, it might be hard to find work that can be done from home. Working from home is not a soft option – you have to be very organized and self-disciplined. You also have to have a fair amount of business acumen, because you'll have to organize your own invoicing, bookkeeping, tax and so on. You'll also have to market yourself – work won't come to you unless you go out to look for it. However, working from home could very well lead on to bigger things; many a company started life on the kitchen table.

A word of warning. You may have seen advertisements in the newspapers asking whether you want to earn lots of money working from home. Liz Hodgkinson points out in *Working Woman's Guide* (1985): 'anybody who advertises "work" is out to get your money, rather than give you any'. Most of the companies that advertise for women working from home are in business to exploit the situation of those confined to the home. By and large, the work is tedious, repetitive and often dangerous. Telephone selling is one of the worst forms of 'commission-only' jobs involving phoning strangers in the evening to try to sell them something such as double glazing, new kitchens or insurance policies. More often than not, you would have to pay for the calls yourself and would only earn anything when you actually made a sale. Party selling is equally dubious and often embarrassing and costly. Pursuing a proper career or job structure if you can would be far more useful and fulfilling.

Part-time work

You may choose to work part-time in order to ease your way back into work or to keep your skills up to scratch. Part-time work is particularly suited to women with children or to those who can't work full-time because of ill health. However, most part-time jobs are poorly paid, low-skill jobs in the service industries. Part-time work is usually paid on an hourly basis and attracts the minimum rate. It is often associated with lack of commitment. The majority of jobs do not carry with them the employment benefits that full-time work has such as being able to belong to a pension scheme, maternity rights, sick pay, paid holidays and so on. However, companies are beginning to turn their attention to part-timers in the light of the shrinking labour force. Some are taking positive steps to appoint part-time workers at higher level jobs and attract them through offering a range of inducements such as training, promotion prospects and other company benefits. One or two companies are encouraging women returners who can only work during term time (students fill in during school holidays).

Job-sharing

Job-sharing is a positive option for many women and signals a commitment to work that perhaps part-time work doesn't. It is a way of working where two people share one full-time job between them. Each sharer does half the work and receives half the pay, holidays and other benefits. Each sharer has her/his own contract of employment but they share the pay and benefits of the full-time post on a pro rata basis. Most people who successfully share a job find that they have to have an equal commitment to the job, be of equivalent seniority, have a good relationship with the sharer and maintain communication outside working hours as well as during a crossover period at work.

All sorts of jobs can be shared and job-sharing is widespread in education, banks, health authorities, factories, local councils, the BBC, the House of Commons and the Civil Service. It is rapidly becoming a valid alternative to the conventional work pattern. A job can be shared in a number of ways – a day can be divided with one partner working mornings, the other afternoons; a week can be divided between two people working two and a half days each; or partners can work alternate weeks. Two people can even work on the same days in the week if that is the busy time for the organization and the other half of the week is quiet. More information on job-sharing can be obtained from the organization New Ways to Work, whose address is at the end of the book. They also keep a job-share register which you can consult if you haven't got an instant partner, and some local careers offices will also have a list of people interested in job-sharing.

Case study

Brenda Hoskyns and **Suzanne Dean** work for a government department and share an executive officer post. They were two of the first people to share a job in their department although a recognized scheme had been operating for some time. It took a few months to negotiate and set up the job-share. Their arrangement is not unusual in that they both work two and a half days a week, Suzanne at the beginning of the week and Brenda taking over at lunch-time on the Wednesday. They either leave themselves time to talk about the work or leave notes for each other. They are lucky in that the work is fairly self-contained and splitting it doesn't cause any continuity problems.

Brenda, who is 58, was coming up to retirement and she felt she wanted to ease off paid work and possibly devote her time to other activities which would increase when she had fully retired. 'This is a very good way of winding down and preparing myself for retirement,' she said. 'So many older people just don't know what to do with themselves once they are retired and many ail as a result.'

Suzanne is 28 and at the other end of the career span. Women often decide to job-share after maternity leave so that they can spend time with younger children but keep a toe-hold on their jobs as well. In Suzanne's case it is a bit different. She doesn't have any children but wanted more time for herself. She is keen on sport and keep-fit and is taking an Open University diploma as well. 'It was quite a struggle getting accepted since I don't have children. People couldn't understand why I wanted to work part-time. I'm very happy with the arrangement now; it gives me the space I want in my private life but it doesn't mean I am not committed to my job. I work hard and go on courses to improve my skills and knowledge as well.'

Flexible working

Flexibility – a key word of the 1990s – has reached the work-place. Many companies are beginning to operate flexible working, perhaps as an alternative to offering child care. There is no reason in principle why everyone should work a five-day, thirty-seven-hour week. In fact, research suggests that people who work a compressed day work harder. Flexible working can be arranged through an agreement between you and your boss about how many days a week you work and what time you start and finish each day. Term-time working was mentioned above and some firms even operate weekend and evening shift patterns to suit women with family commitments but without loss of status or fringe benefits. Flexitime, on the other hand, can take various forms. Usually employees must work a certain number of hours each month but they can vary the time during the day. If an employer operates a core time within a band width (the day's total working time), parents can take children to school in the mornings and still be classed as full-time.

Flexible hours are not the same as flexitime – with some jobs you may be able to work hours that suit you as long as the work gets done. Flexibility may work to your advantage but you need to bear in mind that it may also be used by employers who only need 'casual' labour, and this can be very exploitative of a women's particular situation.

Career breaks

'Career break' is another idea that is gaining popularity as a means of retaining the skills and talent of a trained work-force. Women who have children can of course take maternity leave, which is covered by statute, although some employers may have better terms than others. Some career break schemes allow either parent to take a break of between two and five years after having a baby. A career break can involve returning at regular intervals for updating training or work experience. There may be other reasons for taking a career break, apart from having a baby, such as the desire to travel, writing a book or having to look after an elderly relative. Some careers do not particularly lend themselves to breaks but most do; nursing and teaching spring to mind here. In engineering, many firms are bending over backwards to encourage women to return to their previous jobs and the profession has a number of conversion or updating courses to ease women back to the work-place. Details can be obtained from the Engineering Training Council.

Running a business

The number of women who decide to work for themselves or set up in business has more than doubled in the past ten years. The growth in casual labour and subcontracting has had a lot to do with the increase in this figure. If you can't get a decent job near where you live and which fits in with a family, self-employment maybe the answer. For a mother wishing to combine child care with paid work or for a person who lives a long way from a town or city, it can be an attractive proposition.

Major advantages of working for yourself are independence and freedom, but self-discipline is necessary and a heavy burden of decision-making falls on you. The rewards can be high but so can the stress levels; if things don't turn out well, your entitlement to state benefit is limited. Forming a partnership or a co-operative or employing other people means you are not working alone and this can be rewarding, although it can add complications. A sensible awareness of your own strengths and weaknesses is as vital as assessing the potential demand for your product or service. The personal evaluation quiz on p. 91 (adapted from the *Women Mean Business* directory (1990)) will help you consider how well-suited to self-employment you are.

Do the quiz as quickly as possible; there is no right or wrong answer. There are no scores: the correct answer is the honest one for you.

In *Women Mean Business*, Ivana Cooke has the following advice for women thinking of embarking on the road to tycoonship!

Self-employment typically demands the skills of an account-ant, solicitor, production controller, debt collector, personnel officer, marketing director, sales rep, public speaker and more. Few individuals are extremely creative and superbly organized. You need to know:

What you are good at now

What you can learn or improve

What skills to buy in or hire

No individual can possess all the skills (and time) demanded to maximize business potential: you must delegate and 'let go'.

PERSONAL EVALUATION QUIZ

How well-suited to self-employment are you?

YES Extremely Moderately So-So Moderately Extremely NO

1   Do you have a lot of ideas?
2   Do you find decision-making difficult?
3   Do you plan your day?
4   Are you a good listener?
5   Are you impulsive?
6   Have you experienced stress?
     Was it money related □ or family related □?
     Did you handle it well?
     Did it affect your ability to concentrate?
7   Is your health poor?
8   Do you run your own finances well?
9   Does criticism upset you?
10   Can you delegate tasks to others?
11   Can you talk to strangers easily?
12   Do you like being on your own?
13   Do new challenges worry you?
14   Are you systematic and organized?
15   Can you work long hours?
16   Can you manage other people?
17   Are you a good judge of character?
18   Do you find asking for help/advice difficult?
19   Are you interested in people?
20   Do you always finish boring tasks?
21   Are you prepared to spend time learning new skills?
22   Does being in debt worry you?
23   Do you prefer constant change to routine?
24   Would friends describe you as mainly:
     aggressive □   assertive   □
     passive   □   manipulative   □
25   Do you know your own weaknesses?
26   Reasons for setting up in business.
Tick any which are important to you and double tick any very
important ones:
         More money   □ □
         More leisure   □ □
         Dislike working for other people   □ □
         Money to spend on myself   □ □
         Freedom to work when I choose   □ □
         Higher status   □ □
         More independence   □ □
         Can't get a job   □ □
         Other (specify)   □ □

The responsibility and endless decision-making involved in running your business can be and usually is stressful. Gauge your capacity to cope with reference to stressful situations you have dealt with in the past. As we mentioned in Chapter Two, family support is enormously important. If everyone in your family is opposed to your going it alone, don't. Self-employment can take over your leisure time; be prepared for this and don't expect to make a fast buck overnight; it could take years. It is interesting to note that many 'small' businesses run by women compete successfully with large firms, precisely because they can offer an evening or overnight or weekend service (which of course eats into their leisure or family time).

As a marketing consultant and trainer, Ivana Cooke also offers some wry advice for those who are faint-hearted when it comes to selling:

> Have you ever sold anything to a stranger? As an adviser, I see many people who've been trading about six months. Their friends (and *their* friends!) have bought all the flower-pots/knitwear/redecorating they can bear. To survive, either you or your representative *must* part strangers from their shekels.

You may decide that working in a co-operative would suit you because it would provide a supportive working environment. As a member of a co-operative you jointly own, control and work for the business, share responsibility and make decisions equally, usually receiving equal pay. You need to be able to invest in the company but it is not the same as being self-employed as the firm is usually limited by guarantee. Co-operatives are involved in a wide range of activities such as computing, translating, clothing manufacture, advertising, even child care. Setting up a co-operative is similar to setting up a small business with all the frustrations and occasional crises that this involves, but with the added complications and rewards of working together on a democratic basis.

If you are interested in starting a co-operative business, you should get advice from a co-operative development agency. If there is not one in your locality there may be someone in the Local Authority who specializes in helping people start co-operatives. The Industrial Common Ownership Movement (see Useful Addresses at the back of this book) will also help and advise.

STARTING YOUR OWN BUSINESS

How to get started

1 Find a local need for a product or service, if possible in a field where you have had previous experience.

2 Find out if you can get government support; contact your local TEC.

3 Private sector advice, i.e. bank manager and accountant. Make a friend of both and keep them informed.

4 Seek advice from local planning authority if business is to be at home, i.e. change of use of premises.

5 If you wish to name your business you must register and apply to the Department of Trade and Industry.

6 Watch for sponsored training courses, normally held at technical colleges, i.e. How to start your own business.

7 Think about a health insurance scheme; when health fails the money stops coming in.

8 Keep abreast of all possible new developments in your field. You must avoid stagnation but at the same time do not be tempted to allow your business to expand too quickly; i.e. remember – big is not always beautiful.

9 Use skills of other people when you need them, i.e. secretaries, public relations, printers.

10 Try to gain as much publicity for your business by approaching newspapers or journalists and any other person who could make a story of your success and so give you free advertising. Use this approach as much as possible initially, as advertising is very expensive.

11 Pursue as many channels as possible to market your product or business. Do not be put off initially by thinking that some of these channels may not be of use. Many businesses have been built up as a result of word of mouth.

12 Remember tax will have to be paid on profits – so keep careful records.

13 PERSEVERE.

The business you start up depends on your capabilities and interests but perhaps more importantly on the needs of the market. Do some market research, by which we mean not a costly survey but talking to people you know, look at the area where you live, find out what people need but can't get. You must fix on producing or selling something that fills a gap in the market; you might extend a hobby that you think would make a viable business proposition. This could be something completely new or a new slant on an existing service. You must also work out whether a business would be viable – how much would people be prepared to pay, how many other people offer a similar service, how would you promote your goods or service?

You can get help on these questions and others involved in starting up a business from your local Small Firms Service, local enterprise agencies or Business in the Community and from the local office of the Training Agency or Training and Enterprise Council (TEC). Consultancy services, enterprise training and grants for small businesses are also available. The Enterprise Allowance Scheme (EAS) is open to unemployed people who want to start up a business but to be eligible you have to have been unemployed for at least eight weeks and receiving Unemployment Benefit or Income Support at the time you apply. Ask at your local TEC or Jobcentre about this and about Enterprise Training, which embraces a number of schemes for the newly established business and the self-employed.

Women at work

Having returned to work or perhaps got a job to make ends meet while you are training, it isn't necessarily going to be all plain sailing. The job you land may not be the one you dreamt of, but it is a step on the way. You must expect to feel tired at first; even though housework and looking after children is hard work, being back in the work-place involves a different pace and this might take it out of you for a bit. Your job might involve evening or shift work, which again will be tiring and possibly unsettling. And we all know of the problems women have when they get a job outside the home. Invariably it means a double shift – working eight hours a day in an office, factory or hospital and then coming home to cooking, shopping, ironing and so on. It will take a while to adjust, but don't try to be a superwoman.

If you are lucky enough to find a fulfilling job, you will find you have an increased sense of purpose and self-worth along with new-found energy levels.

At work you will find a new set of acquaintances and friends. Here, too, there will be stresses and strains. We hope we have given you some tools to deal with these. On your side, you have maturity, high-level organizational skills, a lifetime of varied experience of dealing with and caring for people, competence and flexibility. With any luck you will have a sense of humour. But there is still plenty of discrimination against women, and against older women in particular. Unless you organize it otherwise, you'll be the one that always gets asked to make the tea!

Once you have a job, don't stop setting and attaining goals. Plan your career or job moves, plan your training, plan for promotion if that is what you want. Here again, it won't be handed to you on a plate. Unfortunately, it is unlikely you will be recognized for the quality of your work alone. If you are serious about being promoted, you will have to be prepared to learn the rules of the game.

No matter how enlightened the firm you work for is, it is more than likely male-dominated and that means, intentionally or not, male values and rules preside. Men play work games by rules, which they invented and that is why it is they who gain by them and get ahead. You don't have to be aggressive or hang around in pubs to be part of the male fraternity. But you should be aware of male strategies if you are bent on promotion. Increase your visibility. Let people know you are serious about your job. Put your successes or achievements in writing. Let your boss know when you have come back from a training course and tell him/her what you have gained from it, who you made contact with and so on. Look for an opportunity to volunteer to do something. Give people something positive to remember you by.

You should try to make friends with women higher up the ladder, if there are any. Women have been accused of 'pulling up the ladder' once they achieve a certain position rather than giving a helping hand to those who want to climb up. In the past, women have been used to competing for male attention and this has not created any system of solidarity. Hopefully, that is all changing and women have everything to gain from building bridges for each other and creating networks which can be helpful to other women entering the field. There has been growth, in recent years, in the number of women-only professional associations. They allow women to meet and discuss issues that affect their work. These include Women in Manual Trades, Women in Banking and Women in Business.

Sexual harassment may be one such issue. There are a number of books and leaflets on this problem giving advice on how to deal with sexual harassment in the work-place. In larger organizations, the personnel officer should make information available to women, and trade unions also take it seriously and will offer support and advice. Sexual harassment can take a number of forms. You might regard the odd *risqué* remark or joke about women as harmless enough and often men will show off in front of other men in this respect. If you feel that this sort of thing is persistent and increasingly unwelcome and uncalled for, you may find it worth taking up either with the person concerned or someone in authority. If at all possible it is best dealt with firmly but with a sense of humour. You could try ignoring verbal harassment and eventually it will disappear. Or try this technique: if a man at work calls you 'dear' or 'honey' or something you find offensive and demeaning, say to him, 'I know you didn't mean anything by that, but I prefer to be called by my proper name.' He can hardly refuse, and this strategy has the advantage of not being aggressive or trying to score points. As Liz Hodgkinson remarks, 'If you return aggression with aggression, it keeps the game going and can breed antagonism.'

Sexual harassment is hard to combat because women so often defer to men and the man doing the harassing will very often be in a senior position to the woman. It is one further argument for more women reaching positions of responsibility in organizations and bringing about a more equal and democratic culture in the work-place.

5

LEARNING HOW TO LEARN

How to use this chapter

This chapter is designed to help you to learn how to learn. This involves finding out about what is available and making the choices that are right for you. We also believe that a sound understanding of techniques of study appropriate to education and training – and transferable to the world of employment – will enable you to take advantage of a wide range of opportunities. In doing so, you will become confident about yourself and about your own skills and abilities.

Start by looking at the diagram on page 104 which sets out the paths you can follow in education and training. You can then move on to more detailed information which deals with admissions to courses and with grants, fees and allowances, contained in Part I.

Figure 6 (see p. 109) is a guide to the learning techniques set out in Part II and you can see how important the sequence of learning is. For instance, it is unlikely that you will be able to take good notes if your reading and listening skills are not well developed.

If you have had little recent experience of study, it would be advisable to work through Part II step by step, trying out the exercises. For many of them model answers are provided, so that you can begin to get a sense of your own skills and abilities.

However, if you have already been on a course or if you know already where your own strengths and weaknesses lie, you can be more selective. Use the diagram to identify the section(s) you need and then work through them as necessary.

As you acquire new skills or revive those that have been lying dormant, be prepared for change. Learning to take in ideas and information so as to extend your own knowledge is hard and time-consuming work. It affects the way in which your mind works long after the course you were on has finished. The need to think logically and to work systematically, on your own and with others, can have far-reaching effects on you as an individual. It can also change the ways in which family and friends see you. Nevertheless, there are many rewards – both personal and material.

New opportunities in education and training

Statistics can tell us a great deal about women and education, as the graphs in Figure 5 show. As you can see, women more than hold their own in the take-up of places in further education, but are still significantly under-represented in higher education. However, new developments are taking place in both education and training and many of these are aimed at women. Often this has happened because of equal opportunities legislation, but increasingly it is recognized that women have a vital part to play in the economy – if they are given the right kind of education and training. This awareness and the opportunities developing from it are likely to grow rapidly as Britain moves closer to Europe, from 1992 onwards.

WOMEN IN PART-TIME EDUCATION

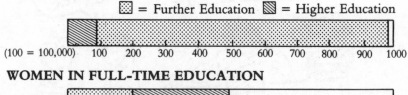

WOMEN IN FULL-TIME EDUCATION

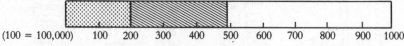

Figure 5 Women in education

Case studies

Here are examples of how the lives of two women from very different backgrounds have changed recently through their involvement with education.

Janet is 27 years old and she was born in England, though her parents come from the Caribbean. She said:

> I used to like school when I was a little girl, but things went wrong for me when I went to the local comprehensive. I lost interest and became very bored, so I left the place as soon as I could.
>
> At first, it was easy for me to earn money, because there were lots of jobs that I could do. I started off as a machinist in a lingerie factory and I made some good friends there. One of them kept on at me to get some qualifications and finally I decided that this was good advice. But it was very hard to work in the daytime and go to classes at night. Then everything got a lot worse and jobs got scarcer and scarcer. I was unemployed for a time and got very depressed.
>
> In 1988, I decided I wanted to start again, so I enrolled for an English course at the local college. I was very nervous and I didn't know anyone. Many of the others in the class were younger than me and I was sure that they were cleverer than me too. But I found out I could still make friends and my confidence began to come

back. I also managed to get a part-time job as a care assistant, looking after nine old ladies. I always did the night shift so that I could get to College in the daytime.

As well as English, I studied Maths, Computing, Typing and Office Practice. My father has been very supportive of me through all this, but several of my old friends tried to put me off. I found this hard to cope with, but I was determined to go on.

Now I am studying full time on an Access Course, because I want to be able to go on and get a degree. I know that if I can get the right qualifications, I shall have a better chance of doing what I want to do. There are still times when I want to run away from it all, just like I have done before. I say to myself I would rather watch television or go out than do my academic work. But I think I have come a long way. I also think that I have a long way to go and I will not give up now.

Enid is 62 years old and, just when she least expected it, her life has changed completely. She wrote:

I left home when I was 16 to train as a nurse and then I joined the ATS. My marriage lasted for thirty-six years, ending with the death of my husband in 1986. By this time, my five children were grown up and settled in homes of their own, leaving me with responsibility for no one but myself. For a while I just drifted, not yet ready for old age, but not knowing what to do.

Then a friend asked me to join a writers' workshop in our village. Although I had always liked letter-writing and had always read a lot, I wasn't very keen. But, after much persuasion, I agreed to go along to the meetings, which were held in the afternoons. I thought I might be able to write a little about my life to give my children some sort of autobiography. Amazingly, the story grew and grew and soon I could not wait to put pen to paper. I began to wish I could do more, but evening classes were out of reach for me because of lack of transport and because of fear of being out after dark in these days of hooliganism.

Then I found out that I could study full-time in a

residential college. After talking the whole thing over with my children, who were behind me all the way, I applied for a place and was accepted. I even got a government grant to cover fees and accommodation!

I have never regretted my decision to study. Apart from the thrill of reading, writing and learning, there is the community life. I have made new friends much younger than I. Before I started the course, I was worried about my ability to take things in. I left school at 14 so I wondered if I was biting off more than I could chew. Well, it was all very different from what I was used to and I have had to work hard. But then, it was much the same for everyone else. It's true that the others were not as old as me, but we were all well distanced from our school days.

Recently, I applied for a place at university to study literature and history and I have been successful. Once again, I am assailed by familiar doubts and worries. The thought of living, working and competing with an even younger generation is very intimidating. But I am absolutely determined to do it.

PART I: OPPORTUNITIES AND INFORMATION

What is possible?

Part-time and full-time courses and training schemes are widely available in towns and cities throughout the country, though provision is scarcer in rural areas. Many preparatory courses are specifically designed with women in mind, especially, for example, in subjects such as engineering, accountancy or physics, where they are in noticeably short supply. Other programmes of study, such as access courses, attract large numbers of women because many offer free or low-cost crèche or nursery places as well as opportunities to learn. Many courses are run inside school hours.

It is really important to make sure that you choose the right course and to do this you will need help. Even then, bear in mind that the world of education and training can change quickly, so that information and advice can soon become out of date. The moral of this is: always check all facts before making a decision.

Before making enquiries, try to decide whether your interests will be best served by education or by training. The former can provide you with a wide range of qualifications at several levels, ranging, for instance, from GCSE to a degree. The latter usually prepares people for a particular occupation such as computer programming, occupational therapy or teaching. Often, employers provide on-the-job training to encourage their workers to update skills or improve prospects of promotion.

Look in your telephone directory for local contacts and addresses, or select from those listed at the end of the book (see Useful Addresses). To help you to make a start, consider the following. (As you do so, bear in mind that it might help you to make a note of the information you want and the questions you need to ask. Of course, it follows from this that you will also want to record the responses that you get.)

Some useful sources of information

Libraries

The reference section of your local library can be a mine of ideas and information. Look for notice-boards, which often display a variety of useful posters and leaflets. Staff are usually very helpful and will answer queries made either in person or over the telephone.

Careers and adult guidance

Each Local Authority runs a centre for advice on educational and training options. On the premises you will find a great deal of information describing courses and routes leading to qualifications and employment. Also specialists are available to deal with adults and this service can include a free private interview where you can assess your aptitudes in relation to your interests.

Unemployment agencies

As well as using the resources described above, look out for Jobclubs and similar provisions, which are to be found in a wide variety of locations. Your first port of call should be the local Jobcentre; although here the emphasis falls upon finding employment, training opportunities are often well publicized.

NEW OPPORTUNITIES IN TRAINING AND EDUCATION

Key questions

Crèche facilities?   Transportation/location?   Hours and duration of course?   Any residential requirements? Equal opportunities for women?   Ethnic minorities and people with disabilities?   Time scales?

Sources of information

Jobcentre   PER   TAPs point   Polytechnics Tertiary colleges   Libraries   Universities   Adult and career guidance services   TECs

Personal objectives

Vocational training?   Voluntary work? Vocational   Qualifications?   Interesting hobby? Full-time and part-time study?

Education		Training	
Part-time	*Full-time*	*Part-time*	*Full-time*
Evening classes	Universities	National	Employment
Adult	Polytechnics	Council for	training
education	Residential	Voluntary	B.Tech.
Access courses	Colleges	Organizations	TECs
	Tertiary	qualifications	
	Colleges	In-service	
		TECs	

Qualifications   Credits   Degrees   Vocational training Employment

Fees, grants and allowances

Local Authority grants   Department of Education and Science   Training agency   Twenty-one-hour rule Charitable institutions   Trade unions   Loans

How long does it take?

Education and training courses occur at certain times within a given year and your ultimate choice could well be influenced by this. Short courses, some of which provide qualifications or credits, can last for a weekend or for several weeks. Substantial part-time study, on an accredited access course for example, is likely to last for a year. Degree or equivalent-level courses last for three years, or four if you are on a sandwich course which involves work placements. But remember that study at this level is calculated on the basis of from thirty-two to thirty-six weeks in attendance, which is then supplemented by a substantial amount of private study carried out in vacation periods.

Education

Most courses, whether part-time or full-time, more or less coincide with school terms (but don't forget to allow for your private study time). The majority of examinations take place in the summer term, which runs from the end of April to the beginning of July. At an early stage, it is worth thinking hard about what methods of assessment would suit you best. For some courses examinations are the only option, but in many others this is combined with continuous assessment of the work you produce as the course progresses. Thus you can go into your exam knowing that you have already earned a proportion of the marks you need for success.

Training

Degree-level courses providing professional qualifications generally observe the calendar described above.

Government-sponsored training courses are funded for limited and specific periods of time. They are often linked to work placements. On-the-job training normally takes place in work time, but it can also include intensive weekend courses.

Admissions

Further education

To join most of the courses available in colleges of further education (now known in many parts of the country as tertiary colleges), you enrol at the beginning of September. Keep an eye on your local newspaper for details or ring up your education office for information.

Higher education

To apply for a place at a university, polytechnic or college of higher education, you normally need to return your application form in the December of the year preceding the one in which you wish to begin your studies. Courses begin in October.

On the form you will need to give details of your past history, including your educational, employment – paid and voluntary – and domestic experience. Many courses have specific requirements for admission, such as certain grades in O Levels, GCSE, A Levels or their equivalents, but often there are exemptions or alternative routes, such as access courses, for adult students. You will also need references, preferably from tutors or previous employers.

Training

The need for training is widely recognized and new opportunities are being developed all the time. Below you will find a brief description of current options, but always make sure you get up-to-date information. (See the list, Useful addresses, at the end of the book.)

If you are registered as unemployed, you are eligible for employment training. This covers a range of training schemes to which you are directed via an action plan. This is a document which profiles your past experience and your current intentions with regard to jobs. Such schemes combine skills training with work placements which are intended to result in paid employment, usually in your own locality. In certain instances, it is possible to move on to courses in further or higher education, if this is seen as a legitimate way to facilitate your action plan. Other options include courses to help you to start your own business and to run it efficiently.

Accreditation

This refers to the value of the qualifications gained as a result of education and training. Those familiar from the past include, for example, O Levels, RSA or City and Guilds. But accreditation itself is changing to accommodate and reflect a series of new developments in education and training.

In further and higher education, many courses are assessed in relation to the new Credit Accumulation and Transfer Scheme (CATS). This incorporates greater flexibility into the award of qualifications by allowing students to gain recognition for part-time as well as full-time study. In this way, the CATS scheme makes it possible to extend the normal three or four years spent on the acquisition of a degree to allow for time which must be spent in employment or in taking on domestic responsibilities.

A similar system is now becoming widely used in adult education, where it is possible to earn credits on a wide range of educational and training courses which have been devised with the needs and aspirations of adult students central to programmes of study. This form of accreditation is usually administered by a number of newly created Open Colleges which have a strong base in the local community, while still achieving national recognition for the quality of the accreditation that they can provide up to the level of entry to higher education.

Options, choices and possibilities continue to change and, overall, to expand. But always make sure that you are working for the qualification which will meet your short- *and* long-term goals.

Funding

This is usually complicated and is often subject to change. In general, grants are available for full-time courses at universities, polytechnics, colleges of higher education and adult residential colleges. Fees are usually charged for part-time courses wherever they are provided, though there are sometimes exemptions if you are registered as unemployed. Training courses often include allowances of various kinds to pay for child care or to cover travelling expenses.

Also it is worth checking on bursaries offered by charitable trusts and by some trade unions to their members. However, this is an area where you should always seek the most detailed information and keep a check on what you are told. Again, keep a written record to refer to in case of difficulty.

Education

The majority of courses in tertiary colleges require you to pay fees for tuition and to register for examinations and/or accreditation, unless you can be exempt because you are registered unemployed. If you are offered a place on the majority of courses in higher education, or at one of the residential colleges which cater for the needs of adult students, you will automatically receive a grant in relation to fees, board and accommodation during term time only. From 1990 onwards, this will be linked to a loan system, operated by the banks, for those on undergraduate courses. Colleges, universities and polytechnics have also been given access funding to assist students in hardship, following upon the abolition of social security and housing benefit. Be sure to enquire (directly to the institution to which you are applying for a place) whether or not you are eligible for help – which you do not have to repay – from this source.

Training

Generally speaking, all government-sponsored training schemes involve the limited provision of allowances and/or travelling expenses. The costs of on-the-job training – expenses, accommodation where necessary, examination fees – are normally borne by your employer.

PART II: LEARNING TECHNIQUES

How to manage your time

The decision to pursue an educational or training course must include a serious consideration of the adjustments which need to be made to ensure that the required work can be carried out in an organized way. Such a decision carries with it a major responsibility for self-direction and may well lead to a whole new lifestyle. The majority of women in such situations are also aware

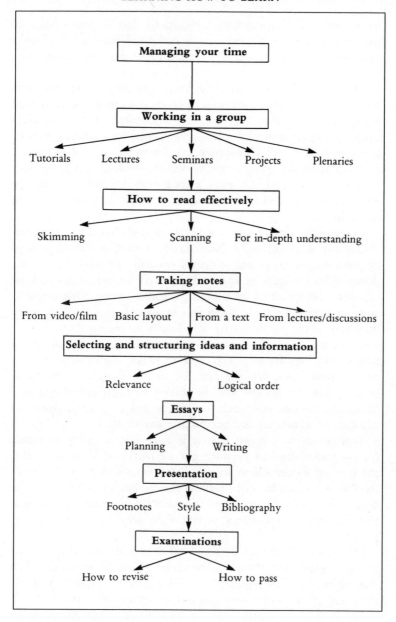

Figure 6 Learning techniques: education and training

of a range of long-standing obligations and responsibilities to partners, parents, children, friends and work-mates. All of these clamour for attention and all of them make demands upon time, as well as energy.

Those who believe that they have very little spare time will have to examine their priorities in relation to their motivation to study or retrain. But, whatever the circumstances, the establishment of a sensible routine which allows time for domestic responsibilities and, where appropriate, employment, as well as leisure, is essential. In this way, everyday decision-making can be reduced to a minimum and this goes a long way towards creating an environment in which new ideas and ways of learning can be taken in.

Everyone is different and it must be said that some temperaments adjust more easily than others to such routines, perhaps because long-term planning comes naturally to them. There are others who see such an approach as likely to stem the free flow of ideas. However, a lack of organization very often leads to wasting valuable time and can also mean that you produce work which is below the standard of which you are capable.

It can also lead to confusion and resentment in the minds of family and friends, who also have to make allowances for your new workload and the commitments arising from it. It must also be said that the person who is willing to drop everything at a moment's notice will rarely be left in peace to settle down to regular, concentrated and productive work!

This is not to suggest that it is ever easy to stick to plans, follow timetables and produce good-quality work on time. But the inevitable temptation to use distractions and domestic problems as an excuse for not studying should be firmly resisted. The best way to do this is to arrive at a workable routine, let everyone else involved know about it and then rely on it as much as possible.

Of course, there will be times when a real crisis disrupts the best-laid plans, but there will be countless other occasions when a good routine will regularly get the very best results out of the time and effort which you can devote to a given task.

Before such a routine can be established, it is necessary to review existing patterns of activity. To do this, keep a diary for a typical week in which all your activities and responsibilities are recorded along with the time they take up. Then examine this to see if it is possible to cut down anywhere on tasks performed and time used. Also think about consulting family and friends to see if they would be willing to co-operate in any way.

It can be equally useful to carry out a similar exercise once your course has begun. Here is an example of a day in the life of Pam, who is studying Sociology at her local tertiary college.

TUESDAY

Activity	Duration	Time
Sleep	8 hours	7.00
Lie in bed	15 mins	7.15
Shower	15 mins	7.30
Search for clothes, then dress	20 mins	7.50
Breakfast for family	20 mins	8.10
Clear away	35 mins	8.45
Do hair, make up	30 mins	9.15
Look for College books (one found finally under daughter's bed)	40 mins	9.55
Walk to bus stop	20 mins	10.15
Wait for bus (chatting)	10 mins	10.25
Journey to College (chatting)	35 mins	11.00
Coffee with friends	30 mins	11.30
Return library books	10 mins	11.40
Hand in essay	10 mins	11.55
Talk to friends over lunch	1 hour	13.25
Wait for lecture to start at		14.00

Pam has been awake and occupied for seven hours before she turns her attention to her studies! Her example is not unusual and it does make a serious point.

Most people in her position would benefit from doing a similar exercise and seeing how much time is used unproductively. Try it for yourself. Here is a checklist to help you to begin to identify your own time-wasters:

• Too many breaks for coffee and tea
• Long telephone conversations
• Unexpected visitors
• Popping out to the shops
• Looking for things that have been mislaid
• Interruptions to your study time
• Watching television
• Not sorting out priorities

111

- Last-minute ironing or mending of clothes
- Avoiding getting down to studies

However, it is difficult to work out a timetable without some idea of the periods to be spent in class or what will be required in private study. But, as a general guide, a full-time course should be seen as being at least the equivalent of a full-time clerical job. People often make the mistake of assuming that all the requirements of a course can be met in class contact time. This is an error which can put you at a disadvantage and limit your potential for success.

It is also easy to underestimate the time required to get to the end of a given piece of work. Certainly, if you are inexperienced be prepared to allow plenty of time for all the stages which lead to completion. Activities such as reading through your work and checking content, structure, style and references take up a surprising amount of time if they are properly carried out. But they also greatly improve the presentation of work and can gain valuable extra marks.

Pacing yourself

Finally, before planning a timetable it is useful to think about the need for rest periods. Physical discomfort and mental indigestion can set in if there is no break. Yet too long a rest can destroy your train of thought and time spent in recovering it is wasted time. The solution is to stop for say ten or fifteen minutes when the pace begins to slow down, when mistakes start to build up or, best of all, when a set target has been reached. Often, a cup of coffee or a snack will be enough to stimulate your flagging energies and work can be continued. At such times, it is often advisable not to become involved with other people or with any distractions. Then your thought processes will continue at a subconscious level and will be readily utilized when work is resumed.

Figure 7 on p. 113 gives an example of a typical timetable for a full-time course, i.e. one which runs for between thirty-two and thirty-six weeks in the year, where terms, to some extent, match those in schools. Can you fit such a pattern of work into your life?

	MONDAY	TUESDAY	WEDNESDAY	THURSDAY	FRIDAY	SATURDAY
9–10	Prepare class paper	Reading for History essay	Shops	Advance reading for lecture (Library)	Read for Communications	Prepare for seminar
10–11		(Library)		Lecture Room 3	Essay (Library)	(Home)
11–12	(Home)	Lecture Room 8				
12–1	Lunch	Lunch	Lunch	Lunch	Lunch	Lunch
1–2	Lecture Room 4	Advance reading for next lecture	Advance reading for next lecture (Home)		Notes for Communications	Laundry
2–3	Books for essay (Library)	Lecture Room 9	Lecture Room 3		Essay (Library)	Cinema
3–4	Break	Break	Break	Student Union Meeting	Break	
4–5	Reading/notes for sociology	General reading	General reading	(Working party afterwards)	Lecture Room 9	
5–6	Start essay (Library)	(Home)	(Home)			
6–7	Dinner	Dinner	Dinner	Dinner	Dinner	Do timetable for next week
7–8	Revise notes for class	Rehearse class paper	Revise notes	Revise notes	Write plan and introduction for	Dinner
8–	Paper (Home)	(Home)	(Home)	(Home)	Essay (Home)	Visit friends/pub

Note: This student chooses not to include Sundays, which are totally occupied by other domestic and family-centred activities.

Figure 7 Typical timetable

113

Group work: education and training

Much of the work done on educational and training courses takes place within a group. Lecturers and trainers are very much aware of the valuable opportunities which this provides. Ideas and information can be disseminated quickly and efficiently to numbers of people. Also, individuals can learn a great deal from each other. They gain confidence from this and from the realization that fears and problems are shared.

Keywords and activities for group work

You might not be familiar with the learning methods used in the education and training programmes devised for people who are over 18 years of age. Here are some definitions and descriptions to help you.

Education

Lectures

These are given by a member of staff and are timetabled for each term. They are designed to provide concentrated information on specific subjects, issues or topics to be taken down in note form. Opportunities for questions or discussion are usually not provided. Lectures last for a minimum of one hour and they can be attended by large numbers of students, e.g. more than a hundred on a popular course at a polytechnic or university.

Things to watch

Initially, many students find the atmosphere in which lectures are given intimidating. They also find it difficult to listen to what is being said and to select and record the required information at the same time.

Seminars

These are discussion groups whose meetings are regularly timetabled throughout the term. Usually a member of staff controls the group in an informal way. Preparatory reading is often required and extracts from set texts or other relevant documents are frequently the subject of discussion. Your notes can provide a record. They might also provide valuable material for written work or revision.

On some courses, each person is asked to prepare and present a class paper to the rest of the group. These are written on specific topics and provide a focus for group discussion. They are often taken in by the tutor for assessment after the seminar.

Things to watch

Discussion can be far-ranging and seemingly (or actually) unstructured. Communication skills and levels of knowledge and confidence can vary enormously and this can be distracting. Also, it can be difficult to join in the discussion and to take notes of what is important. The real value of this experience is likely to become apparent to you only after reflection. Quick results should not always be expected!

Group tutorials

Usually, these occur only once or twice each term and provide opportunities for a group of three or four students to discuss their work with a member of staff. Essays and assignments are often handed in for marking before the tutorial. They are assessed and handed back at this meeting. Group tutorials can be a very useful learning experience because it is possible to see how others – including you – are making progress.

Things to watch

Individual strengths *and* weaknesses are revealed to the rest of the tutorial group. Also, competitive feelings can develop in the group.

Group projects

Some courses include projects as part of assessed work. Two or three people work together to complete a given task which will be presented jointly. This allows for the division of labour and enables each person to identify and use her/his individual skills and abilities in a co-operative way.

Things to watch

Common objectives and methods of working can be hard to establish and maintain. Also, it can be difficult to ensure that the work is divided fairly and that the contributions of each individual gains due recognition.

Training

Discussion groups

In the main, these are attended by two groups of people:

1 personnel from one section or department;
2 representatives from a variety of companies, sections or departments.

Trainees are involved in a series of discussions and other practical activities relevant to the work-place situation. One or more trainers will organize the group and monitor performance.

Things to watch

The direct connection between work and training can set up a stimulating but competitive atmosphere. Also, the nature of some training objectives involves challenging established working practices and the attitudes and beliefs upon which they are based.

Feedback sessions

These can take place between the trainers and the whole group of trainees or separate small groups, or between trainer and individual trainee. The strengths and weaknesses of achievement at all levels are discussed and advice for the future is normally given.

Things to watch

As above.

Plenary sessions

These require reports on specific subjects and activities from representatives of small groups or from individuals. Opportunities for questions and comments on the training programme are usually provided.

Things to watch

Reports must accurately represent what has happened and this can be difficult to achieve on an intensive training course. Also, speaking to a large peer group can be a daunting prospect. Make sure that your report *does* accurately represent what has been said. Pay special attention to presentation in written form. If you are nervous or inexperienced in making verbal reports, make the time to rehearse what you are going to say. Pitch your voice so that it can be heard easily and time your presentation. Be prepared to put in extra work to make a good impression!

Checklist of skills for group work in education and training

- Listening skills
- Speaking skills
- Note-taking skills
- Ability to complete preparatory work
- Ability to use preparatory work effectively
- Ability to achieve a good standard of spoken and written communication

Effective reading

The ability to read effectively is an essential requirement for success on educational and training courses. Most of us can make sense – without too much difficulty – of the things that we read as part of everyday life. We read to our children, to follow a recipe or to use a timetable to see when the train leaves the station. But reading as part of a course needs careful consideration if vital learning objectives are to be achieved.

Many enthusiastic but inexperienced students believe that they must read every single word of their material to gain maximum understanding. Consequently, reading is a slow and laborious process which takes a great deal of time. Also, all written material is treated in the same way, whether or not it is relevant to the task in hand. This approach reduces the reader to a passive recipient of

117

ideas and information, and this is a position which hinders rather than encourages intellectual progress.

How to read effectively

- Establish clear objectives – note briefly exactly what you are looking for before you start.
- Set aside time when you will not be interrupted.
- Be prepared to use a variety of reading techniques as set out below.

An appropriate understanding of reading material is based on the ability to use three basic techniques, which can be described as follows.

Skimming

This is a survey of the material which is done very quickly by allowing the eyes to move rapidly over the page, with the attention directed towards the recognition of titles, names, dates, figures and so on.

This technique encourages quick identification of format as well as general content. For example, it is easy, at a glance, to recognize a poem as opposed to an extract from a novel, or a policy document as opposed to a page from a training manual.

Scanning

This type of reading uses the technique described above but it has two objectives – *to locate* and *to identify* specific kinds of information and ideas such as keywords, lines of argument or other essential material. These key elements can be underlined or highlighted on the text. (Library books or other similar material will require brief notes made on additional paper.)

Intensive reading

This technique should not be seen as a substitute for either skimming or scanning even though it depends upon the ability to identify and select relevant ideas and information which are the basic objectives of both those methods. But, in addition, intensive reading requires the ability to recognize what is implied through the network of unstated associations which cluster around key concepts.

At this point, it is important to emphasize that this level of understanding is not derived only from what is read. To a large extent, it draws upon the knowledge and experience which grows as progression through a course takes place. It builds upon the wealth of perceptions, reactions, ideas and information which multiplies as learning occurs and understanding is achieved.

The development of the necessary analytical skills which lead to this kind of comprehension is encouraged by the adoption of a critical – as opposed to a passive – approach to what is being read. So, as well as reading with the objectives of selecting, recording and absorbing, as efficiently as possible, the ideas and information presented by the writer, the reader takes on another task. This is to identify complex or ambiguous or contradictory arguments and concepts. These occur in many learning situations. For example, they could be found on a training course which was designed to encourage employees to consider how changes in company policy will affect practice. They may also arise when the reader is confronted with differences of interpretation or con-troversial opinions expressed by various authorities in, for instance, the study of sociology or history. Once the existence of these complexities has been recognized, the reader is in a position to tease out the deeper implications contained in written material. It is also possible to identify the means by which writers structure and present complicated ideas and concepts and to con-sider the implications arising from them.

Exercises

Try out the skimming and scanning techniques that you have just read about. Model answers against which you can measure your own work are provided on p. 122.

How to do it

1 Read through the passage very quickly, allowing your eyes to focus on names, dates, numbers and any keywords with emerge. Mark or note these down on a separate sheet of paper as you go.

2 Write down a suitable title for what you have read. (This will show the level of understanding achieved.)

Skimming: extract 1

You may have become aware that at work or at home you feel continually tired and edgy, and that you are losing your temper more often – in fact that you are becoming stressed. Busy people of high intelligence and sensitivity are most susceptible to this. The consumption of sedatives, tranquillisers, pain killers, alcohol, tobacco and coffee increases yearly. In 1979 a total of 41.85 million prescriptions for tranquillisers, sedatives and hypnotics was issued in the United Kingdom at a cost of £43.98 million.

Possibly you suffer from persistent chest pains, tummy pains or even ulcers, asthma or skin disorders, and your doctor may have told you to try and relax to help these conditions. Figures for killer diseases, in which stress is a contributing factor, are really frightening. Deaths in England and Wales from coronary heart disease were 805 per million for men and 348 per million for women in 1941. Thirty years later these had shot up to 2,603 and 1,579 respectively.

Laura Mitchell, *Simple Relaxation*
(John Murray, 1985) p. 13

Scanning: extract 2

Mr E. M. Forster's title *A Room with a View* is symbolical, of course; and to explain the sense in which he conveys it will introduce our comments also. Lucy Honeychurch and her elderly cousin Charlotte go to stay at a pension in Florence; their rooms, they grumble, have no view. A gentleman promptly exclaims, 'I have a view; I have a view', and proceeds to offer them his room and that of his son George. They are outraged, but they consent; and when cousin Charlotte has insisted that she should occupy the young man's apartment, because he is a bachelor, she discovers, pinned over the washstand 'an enormous note of interrogation'. 'What does it mean? she thought . . . Meaningless at first, it gradually became menacing, obnoxious, portentous with evil.' But if we are not cousin Charlotte, in age or temper, if, moreover, we have read what Mr Forster has written in the past, we are amused rather than bewildered. We are more than amused, indeed, for we recognise that odd sense of freedom which books give us when they seem to represent the world as we see it. We are on the side, of course, of Mr Emerson and his son George, who say exactly what they mean. We care very much that Lucy should give up trying to feel what other people feel, and we long for the moment when, inspired by Italy and the Emersons, she shall burst out in all the splendours of her own beliefs. To be able to make one thus a partisan is so much of an achievement, the sense that one sees truth from falsehood is so inspiring, that it would be right to recommend people to read Mr Forster's book on these accounts alone. If we are honest, we must go on to say that we are not so confident by the time the book is at an end.

Virginia Woolf,
a review of *A Room with a View* (E. M. Forster)
(*Times Literary Supplement*, 22 October 1908)

Model answers

Skimming: extract 1

Possible titles: Stress
Effects of stress
Stress and illness

You may have become aware that at work or at home you feel continually tired and edgy, and that you are losing your temper more often – in fact that you are becoming **stressed**. Busy people of high intelligence and sensitivity are most susceptible to this. The consumption of sedatives, tranquillisers, pain killers, alcohol, tobacco and coffee increases yearly. In **1979** a total of **41.85 million prescriptions** for **tranquillisers**, sedatives and hypnotics was issued in the **United Kingdom** at a cost of **£43.98 million**.

Possibly you suffer from persistent chest pains, tummy pains or even ulcers, asthma or skin disorders, and your doctor may have told you to try and relax to help these conditions. **Figures** for **killer diseases**, in which **stress** is a contributing factor, are really frightening. **Deaths in England and Wales** from coronary heart disease were **805 per million for men** and **348 per million for women** in **1941. Thirty years later** these had shot up to **2,603** and **1,579** respectively.

Scanning: extract 2

Possible titles: The story of *A Room with a View*
The meaning of *A Room with a View*
Virginia Woolf's interpretation of *A Room with a View*

Key themes and ideas   The connections between the Emersons and Lucy Honeychurch
The importance of Lucy learning to trust her own feelings
The relationship between fiction and real life

How to take notes

The ability to take brief and accurate notes is a vital skill which, like effective reading, is essential to success in educational and training courses. The majority of participants soon become aware of the value of making their own personal record of the wide range of valuable and thought-provoking ideas, facts and figures presented to them on courses via books, lectures, discussions and videos. Indeed, good notes are the basic raw material from which both conceptual understanding and successful written work are derived.

In a lecture or a discussion, however, those new to this essential skill often make the mistake of trying to write down *everything* they hear as quickly as possible. When faced with a jumbled, incomplete and often totally confused record, they blame this upon their inability to use shorthand, or they may consider taping such sessions as a substitute for taking notes.

Such conclusions reveal a fundamental misunderstanding of the function of note-taking. Shorthand or tape-recording would only provide a literal record of the given subject-matter, whereas good notes provide a *brief, accurate and selective* account of relevant material.

Taking notes both develops and demands a real understanding of source material. It is worth mentioning again the importance of using effective reading techniques, which is the means by which this process of learning begins. It is also important, at this stage, to make a distinction between taking notes from written sources and from lectures, discussions or videos. The rapidity of speech and the added complication of images allows little time for thought and the note-taker's responses have to be almost immediate. Keywords, phrases and ideas have to be selected, arranged and recorded at speed and so it is suggested that attention is directed first to taking notes from the printed word. But, whatever the subject-matter, be clear about what the process of note-taking involves as a *mental* and *analytical activity*. This is set out in Figure 8.

Designing your notes

As in most activities, attention to basic organization – in this case, a consistent layout for your notes – can save valuable time

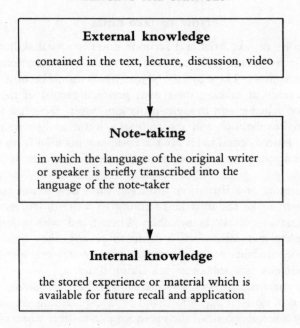

Figure 8 The process of note-taking (Source: Pat Heaton and Gina Mitchell, *Learning to Learn*, Bath: Educational Publishers, 1987)

in the long run. It can soon become something to rely upon automatically, leaving the mind free to concentrate upon the selection of new ideas and information. Here are some suggestions for you to try out in the exercise which you will find below.

Basic layout

1 Note the date of the lecture, seminar, discussion group, video screening, plenary discussion or meeting.
2 Create a title to represent broadly the subject-matter, areas to be covered, problems to be considered.
3 Accurately note the full title of a book, e.g.

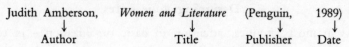

Judith Amberson,   *Women and Literature*   (Penguin,   1989)
Author   Title   Publisher   Date

4 Accurately note the page numbers from which you take notes or direct quotations. This is essential for essay-writing and for footnotes.

Organization

1 Allow plenty of space for later additions by leaving broad margins on either side of the page and by writing on one side only.
2 Work out a clear system for classifying the information you select, e.g. use Roman numerals (I, II, III, IV, V) or capital letters (A, B, C, D, E) for main points and Arabic numerals (1, 2, 3, 4, 5) and small letters (a, b, c, d, e) for minor or supporting points.
3 Use a red pen to underline keywords, names or dates or to otherwise mark out items of special importance.
4 Use abbreviations to save time and speed up writing.

Abbreviations

Certain terms and expressions are used repeatedly on every course and it is useful to develop your own personal shorthand for them. Also, listed below are some commonly used abbreviations. Try them out and practise them until they become familiar. Do not leave it until you attend your first lecture!

$\therefore$	therefore
$\because$	because
$>$	greater than
$<$	less than
$=$	equals, is same as
$\neq$	does not equal, is not same as
e.g.	for example
NB	this is important, take notice
i.e.	that is
wd	would
cd	could
b/4	before
v	versus
$+$	also, in addition to

Exercises

Try out your ability to take notes and to work out your own
layout for them on the following extracts. You will find model
answers on p. 128. The first one will demonstrate the line-by-
line form of notes, the second will use a spider diagram. This is
a very useful method of recording information and ideas from
lectures as well as from books and articles. However, you should
practise the line-by-line method thoroughly before moving on to
the more advanced diagrammatic form.

Extract 1

French police now apply road laws strictly and are much
tougher about speeding than our police. Speed traps abound,
fines are heavy for any breach of the law, rise with increased
speed, and are collected on the spot. So French drivers are
much more careful than they were and resent foreigners who
are not (especially Belgians!). But they do not always keep
to the 130 kph (81 mph) on the toll motorways unless they
suspect that the police are about. Speed limits are 60 kph (38
mph) in town, 90 kph (56 mph) outside town, 130 kph (81
mph) on dual carriageways. You must have headlamps
altered to dip right. French motorists also object if your
beams are not yellow. Do both jobs by using yellow plastic
lens covers or plastic stick-ons with yellow paint provided.
The A.A. reminds us regularly that few Britons are used to
driving more than 250 miles a day during the working year;
100 miles is enough for one stretch without a rest or walk.
That applies to passengers as well as drivers, so switching
drivers and pressing on does little to help you or your car.
The French have 'fatigue' zones. They reckon that Beaune,
200 miles from Paris on the motorway, becomes a driver
'fatigue zone'. That is where those coaches packed with
children crashed in summer 1982.

Arthur Eperon, *Encore –
Traveller's France* (Pan, 1983) p. 15

Extract 2

Are attitudes to food likely to change in the future? In recent years perhaps we have become too closely involved with the presentation of food, concentrating on the table, the china and the flowers in a restaurant – instead of thinking seriously about what we eat.

In the coming decade, economic and ecological factors could combine to remind us that we all depend on food for our very survival. If the advertising industry gets hold of this idea, the notion of 'survival food' might become trendy! If we all saw food as a vital source of life, it would have a profound effect on how we filled our shopping bags. Ingredients would be chosen and prepared according to different standards, as their contribution to the prolongation of life was carefully weighed and measured by cooks and by those who consumed their dishes.

All known and potential sources of food would be closely examined with a view to establishing nutritional content. Such an approach could draw upon the precedents set in the Second World War when scarce resources were rationed. In spite of this, men, women and children were said to have been better fed and consequently healthier than in peacetime!

Taken from unpublished essay by Linda Brooke,
'Food and the Environment'

Model answers

Extract 1

Notes on A. Eperon, *Encore – Traveller's France*
Date: (Pan, 1983) p. 15

Holiday driving in France

I.   France – speed laws tougher than UK.
II.   E.g. strict limits inside towns (38 mph), outside (56 mph) + dual carr.
      toll roads (81 mph)
III. BUT French sometimes exceed on toll roads.
IV.   Headlamps dip right + yellow
V.   English not drive >100 miles = passengers same

Extract 2: in the form of a spider plan

Food and the Environment: L. Brooke

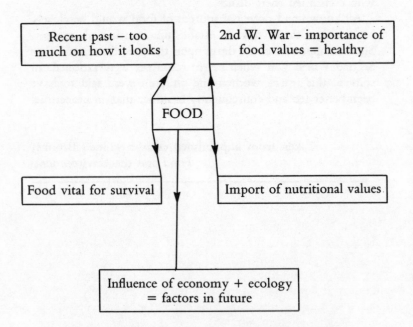

How to take notes from TV, video or film

We live in a society which is increasingly dominated by visual

128

images. Nearly every home contains a television set and many people now own video-recorders. So it is hardly surprising that those working in the world of education and training have been quick to take advantage of a new technology which adds variety and topicality to their teaching programmes. Students too often feel that taking in ideas from a familiar screen instead of from the printed word, for example, will be easy.

However, if maximum benefit is to be derived from these new learning opportunities, problems arising from their use must be faced. In fact, familiarity with the screen can itself put obstacles in the way of achieving the concentration necessary for the efficient absorption of information. For instance, for most of us the TV screen is in the living-room and is rarely the centre of undivided attention. Other activities are being carried on and usually we respond only briefly and intermittently to programmes which we think of as providing us primarily with entertainment. Obviously such attitudes and the viewing patterns coming from them are likely to be counter-productive to the learning process.

It is also important to realize that recording information from the screen can make even more demands upon us than taking notes from a lecture, because of the added impetus of the visual imagery which accompanies the commentary. Nevertheless, the input from video, TV or film needs to be absorbed, recorded and used with just as much care as that from other sources, if it is to serve the purpose for which it is included in a course.

For this to happen, always ensure that you understand the relationship between screenings and the rest of your course. In this way, you can adopt a positive approach to this method of learning which is comparable to that recommended in the section on reading techniques.

The best way to confront the problem of making notes – and thus taking eyes off the screen – can be tackled by using the diagrammatic style demonstrated in the spider plan model answer set out on p. 128. Essentially this technique relies upon the selection of keywords, issues and concepts which can be written down very briefly. Also, the spider plan format allows space for the alignment of ideas and information and for later additions. Spending a few minutes reviewing what has been noted in this form can be extremely valuable, for it often results in a significant improvement of understanding and in the retention of what has been learned.

However, it must be emphasized that this technique needs to be practised thoroughly before it can be relied upon in the real-life situation. Fortunately, this is easy to do.

Practising spider plans

1 Persuade a friend or a member of your family to read out a suitable piece from a newspaper or magazine and make a spider plan.
2 Compare what you have created against the original as soon as it is completed.
3 Leave the work for 24 hours, then look again at your spider plan and see how much you can remember of the original source material. You are likely to be pleasantly surprised at how much you understand and how much you have retained!
4 Similar opportunities for practice can be found by taking notes from a TV news programme or documentary.
5 If working alone, success can be measured against your own recollections of the original material.

Selecting and structuring ideas and information

As the experience of study grows and people become more confident of their own abilities, many of them come to realize that they can use appropriate reading and note-taking techniques quite comfortably. Consequently, they find the task of collecting material relatively easy. However, difficulties commonly arise in relation to the need to put the information collected in sets of notes into a logical order. This is essential if a satisfactory standard of communication is to be achieved between the writer of a given assignment, project or essay and the person who is going to read and assess it. Here is an exercise to help you to do this.

Exercise: selecting and structuring

1 Begin by assuming that you have collected certain items of information about the subject of your essay, Elizabeth James.
2 This is collected together in various sets of notes, which must be organized logically so as to provide the basis of your essay.
3 Read through the information set out below (in deliberately random order).
4 Select all the important items and reject any which are of minor significance.

5 Arrange your selection so that it gives the story of Elizabeth's life and is easy to read and understand.
6 Write it out so that it communicates easily.
7 Compare with the model answer on pp. 132 to 133.

Notes on the history of Elizabeth James

- In 1895, Hubert Blenkiron secured an engagement as a singer at the Newcastle Empire and then left for London with a touring theatrical company, promising to send for Elizabeth soon.
- Elizabeth and Hubert were divorced in 1910.
- Increasingly between 1900 and 1909, Hubert's understudy was required to take his place on stage.
- Elizabeth Mary Hannah James had red hair and she was born in a small village called Marten in 1872.
- Marten was a coal-mining village nine miles from Newcastle upon Tyne. In the 1980s, long after Elizabeth's death, the last pit closed and the character of Marten changed altogether. Young people moved away to find employment and most of those remaining lived in reduced circumstances on redundancy payments and then on social security.
- Elizabeth was imprisoned in Holloway for three weeks in 1904 on a charge of disturbing the peace.
- In 1894, Elizabeth became engaged to Hubert Arthur Blenkiron, who was the son of the village blacksmith in Marten.
- Accompanied by her mother, she went down to London to visit Hubert in January 1897, when he was in pantomime at the Victoria Palace.
- Even at the height of his fame, newspaper stories frequently hinted at Hubert's fondness for strong drink.
- Hubert soon began to make a reputation as a singer in musical comedy, being less successful as a straight actor.
- Elizabeth died of influenza in 1919.
- Elizabeth adopted two children from a charitable foundation.
- Hubert's contract to star as male lead in *The Merry Widow* at the Haymarket was cancelled unexpectedly amid a buzz of speculation at the end of 1909.
- The marriage took place in London in October 1987 and after that Elizabeth lived most of her life in London.

- Elizabeth visited Marten only four times after her marriage, once for her mother's funeral in 1907.
- Elizabeth had no children of her own.
- Elizabeth became involved in charitable work in the East End of London and was particularly well known in Whitechapel.
- In 1903, she became active in the Suffragette movement.
- At first, Elizabeth received letters frequently from Hubert.

Model answer: the life and times of Elizabeth James

Elizabeth was born in Marten, a small coal-mining village near Newcastle upon Tyne in 1872. She moved to London in 1897, when she married Hubert Blenkiron. Hubert came from Marten too, but left and eventually became a star of musical comedy on the London stage.

Elizabeth seemed to make up her mind quickly to adjust to life in London. She went back to Marten rarely, but she did return briefly for her mother's funeral in 1904. Evidence suggests that Elizabeth had little or nothing to do with Hubert's career. She occupied herself in charitable work and was particularly well known in Whitechapel.

Hubert became increasingly successful, but even at the height of his fame, when his name was frequently mentioned in the Press, there were hints that he was drinking to excess. As time went by, there were occasions when Hubert was unable to appear and his place at a particular performance was taken by his understudy.

For her part, since no children were born of the marriage, Elizabeth approached a charitable organization and adopted two orphans. She also took an interest in politics and began to work with the Suffragettes. She was very active and was imprisoned in Holloway for three weeks in 1904, the year of her mother's death.

Her marriage to Hubert ended in divorce in 1910 and it is only possible to speculate about the reasons for this turn of events. One factor which may be of significance is that Hubert's career came to a sudden and unfortunate end in 1909, when his contract to appear in *The Merry Widow* was suddenly cancelled. Influence may also have been exerted by what seems to have been his growing addiction to alcohol. Elizabeth's political interests and activities may also have played a part in bringing about the break-up. Elizabeth's life came to an end in 1919, when she died of influenza at the age of 46.

How to write essays

Tutors ask students to write essays for the following reasons:

- to see what they have learnt from their studies;
- to see whether students understand what is relevant to the question;
- to see how well selected ideas and information can be handled;
- to see how effectively written work is organized;
- to see whether the English language is used correctly.

However, there is no perfect, ideal or model way to write an essay. This is because essay questions are related to particular courses and to particular academic disciplines. Also the people who write essays are all individuals. We all write – as we speak – in a highly individual way. The following guidelines are not intended to change this situation. But it is possible to identify certain methods which, if put into practice, will result in a well-structured and well-written essay.

Vocabulary

Essays focus upon the written word as the central means of communication between writer and reader. It is also worth noting that most essays also require the use of formal language. Both of these factors have the effect of extending vocabulary. This is one of the most valuable parts of the learning experience and recent research has shown that a limited command of language is a severe disadvantage in all subjects. This is because the ability to reason, which is vital for personal and intellectual development, is hampered by a restricted vocabulary.

So do not allow yourself to be daunted by the need to use new words in specialized ways. Remember that by the age of 12 most children have about 12,000 words at their command and a vocabulary of the same size meets the needs of most adults. A popular newspaper requires a reading age of an average 8-year-old! Compare this with the fact that most graduates have a vocabulary of some 23,000 words and draw your own conclusion about the value of increasing your own word power.

133

Style and the conventions of essay-writing

The following points will help you to reach a good standard of presentation. Experience indicates that it is useful to be aware of specific practical information of this kind, before settling down to the task of planning and writing a complex and demanding piece of work.

Basic requirements

- All essays should include the full title at the top of the first page and it should be underlined.
- Pages should be numbered and they should have margins.
- Your writing should be either double-spaced (i.e. write on a line, miss a line) or on one side of the page only. This is to allow space for your tutor's comments.
- Don't forget to add your name.

Contractions

- In general, avoid shortening words. For instance, instead of 'don't', write 'do not' and so on.

Numbers

- Numbers up to one hundred should be written out in words.
- Beyond one hundred, use figures.
- Specific quantities should also appear in figures, e.g. 5 kilos, 10 metres, 15 per cent.

Quotations

- Remember that tutors are interested in *your* words so use quotations sparingly.
- Quotations of up to about forty words in length can be incorporated into the running line of your writing, using quotation marks as follows:

The Prime Minister discussed problems 'facing those women of all ages who wished to equip themselves to compete in the changing job market'. She went on to consider other factors relating to the economy, and expressed concern about the current balance of trade.

- Longer quotes should be indented, i.e. written out in lines about an inch shorter on either side than the rest of your text, as follows:

It was felt that courses designed primarily for women had been successful. A lecturer from the Polytechnic said that women attending the reunion:
> had gone on to do all sorts of things. Some of them had gone straight into jobs, many had gained really good qualifications. In one evening, I came across a civil servant, a vet's assistant, a bank manager, a playgroup organizer, a florist, an occupational therapist, a primary school teacher, a market researcher, a computer programmer, a home help and a psychologist.

Titles

- All titles of publications (e.g. books, plays, pamphlets), films and so on should be underlined, and titles of articles, chapters, poems, etc. should be enclosed within quotation marks. (Remember to apply this to the titles of your own work.)

Bibliographies

- A bibliography is a list of all the sources used and it should appear at the end of your essay.
- You can achieve a good effect if you set out your material in sections to cover books, articles, newspapers and so on.
- List them all in alphabetical order by authors' surnames as follows:

Bergson, R. <u>Women Returners in the 1990s</u> (Penguin Books, 1989)

Crispin, F. <u>Patterns of Inequality</u> (Methuen, 1986)

Davidson, G. <u>New Opportunities for Women</u> (Pan, 1981)

| Author | Title (underlined) | Publisher or place of publication | Date of publication |

Footnotes

- Footnotes show from where you took your quotations.
- In advanced work, they can also be used to provide summaries of information relevant to your essay but too large to be conveniently incorporated into the text of it.
- Footnotes can be added at the bottom of the pages to which they refer or they can be inserted on a separate page at the end of your essay.

Example

An important piece of research on educational opportunities in British universities and polytechnics has just been published. Its authors are concerned to point out 'some of the new developments which are influential in assisting those involved in higher education to face up to the demands of the economy'.[1]

In this context, the position of women is of prime importance. This issue is the subject of a new book also published this year which takes as its theme the need to provide adequate support for those women who aim to combine family responsibilities with full-time study.[2]

1 W. F. Graham and T. Jenkins, *Higher Education and The Economy: The Need for Change* (London, 1990) p. 14.
2 See M. James, *Education and the Needs of Women* (Oxford, 1990).

Abbreviations

You will often find that you need to refer more than once to the same source, when you are writing up your essay. When this happens, you should make use of the following abbreviations in footnotes. They will save you time and they add a professional touch to your work. Also, if you know how to use these abbreviations yourself, you will be able to understand what they refer to when you come across them in your reading.

Ibid.

This is short for *ibidem* and it is Latin for 'in the same place'. It is used when a second reference to a source follows immediately after the first one, as follows:

1 M. Eagleton and D. Pierce, *Attitudes to Class in the English Novel* (London, 1979) p. 43.
2 Ibid., p. 117.

op. cit.

This is short for *opere citato* and it is Latin for 'in the work quoted'. At first glance, you might think that this is not really any different from 'ibid.', but there is an important distinction in that 'op. cit.' is used only when other references have intervened. When this happens, there is a gap between the first full reference and the one footnoted as 'op. cit.'. So the reader is obviously going to need more information to locate the original source. To assist in this, it is usual to insert the author's surname before 'op. cit.'. Here are some examples:

1 M. Eagleton and D. Pierce, *Attitudes to Class in the English Novel* (London, 1979) p. 43.
2 Ibid., p. 117.
3 F. Weldon, *Letters to Alice* (London, 1984) p. 26.
4 Eagleton and Pierce, op. cit., p. 88.

Planning and writing the essay

In general, essays are directly related to course work. This means that you should be able to see the relationship between the essay title and the seminar groups and lectures you have attended and the reading you have already done.

You are normally provided with a list of essay titles from which to make your choice and this list includes a bibliography for each essay. Resist the temptation to plunge straight into the reading list, with a view to reading everything it contains! Remember that you are required to demonstrate your ability to *select information which is relevant to your title*. So think hard about what the question is asking you to do using the following method.

Stage one: approaching the question

- Begin by underlining the key words and phrases in the question.
- Then write down all the ideas, topics, facts and issues that you can think of which are at all relevant to your question. (Spider plans are very useful for this.)

Stage two: structure and organization

Essays must have a structure and this is achieved by working out a plan on which your essay will be based. Well-planned essays attract higher marks, but there is another advantage too. This method of working cuts out all the time that you can waste waiting for inspiration, or wondering what to write after the first sentence and the second and the third . . .

Stage three: making the plan

- All essays should include: an introduction;
  the main body – ideas, facts,
  themes, analysis;
  the conclusion.

- Review all the ideas you have noted down in stage one and decide on what to include and what to omit.
- Arrange your selected material under the main sections set out above. At this stage, you will often find it helpful to use headings and subheadings. (These do not usually appear in the finished work.)
- Use these headings to help you to make your selections from the reading list.
- When you read, remember to make notes.
- Use your notes to flesh out your original plan, adjusting it as necessary.
- Always remember that you are writing for someone else to read and that things which seem obvious to you may not be so clear to another person.

Using the plan

The introduction

Build upon your notes to set the scene for what is to come:

- Make your intentions plain.
- Provide your reader with a clear context for what you are writing.
- Do not make assumptions.

Sample introduction

If you are writing an essay entitled 'The Disadvantaged Child: the Effects of Social Deprivation', do not assume that everyone shares your idea of 'disadvantaged'. Define all keywords so that your reader is aware from the beginning of your terms of reference.

You could begin like this:

> The term 'disadvantaged' has many different associations and interpretations. Broadly, it is seen to mean privations suffered by adults as well as children. However, the description of a 'disadvantaged child' is defined much more specifically in the context of government reports. In such documents, it is clear that a disadvantaged child is one who is nurtured in an area of high unemployment, inadequate health care and schooling, and poor housing.
>
> This essay will focus upon one such child, Tracy D., who fits into all these categories. Her history is contained in reports written by a number of social workers, but the following account is based on information supplied by her mother.
>
> Tracy was born in April 1982 and was the third child of her mother's second marriage.

Main body

This is always the longest single section of an essay and needs to be planned with care. Develop your notes and build up paragraphs here (and all through your writing) to structure your ideas. Bear in mind that:

- Sentences usually convey single thoughts.
- Paragraphs are made up of groups of thoughts which are contained in sentences. These are then arranged in sequence so as to communicate clearly.
- Usually the opening sentence in a paragraph is the key to what is to follow.
- Those which follow on develop the idea, topic or theme by providing more information and completing the message to the reader.
- The opening sentence in a paragraph can also be used to build

in some signposts for your reader to follow as the direction of your writing changes, like this:

At this point it is important to note that . . .

Having considered the causes of this particular problem, some attention must now be given to its effects . . .

- At the end of a paragraph, look back at your title and make sure that you are not wandering from the point.

Conclusion

A satisfactory conclusion should gather together all that has been said so that your reader is left with a summary of your subject and your arguments. If you cannot reach a definite decision about an issue, it might be appropriate to indicate what further research in the field is needed. But always make sure that this approach is acceptable in relation to your course work and to your title.

The final stage

- Always be prepared to make several drafts of an essay, especially if you are inexperienced.
- Editing your own writing is an important part of the learning process and contributes a great deal to personal and intellectual development.
- Allow ample time for this work.
- Read your essay out loud to locate repetitions and gaps in content or argument.
- Check for errors in spelling, punctuation and general use of English.
- Check all footnotes and your bibliography for accuracy.

Dealing with examinations

Everyone feels nervous at the prospect of taking an examination. Examiners are aware of this and often comment upon the way in which many candidates do not do justice to their obvious abilities. Some do not read the examination paper properly and so do not do what they are asked. Others run out of time and fail to finish all the questions, though the answers that they do manage to complete may reach a very high standard. However, examination results are usually worked out on the basis of *average marks* and this means that unanswered questions pull down final results.

However, if you adopt a positive mental attitude based on the belief that a course is designed to lead you through your study programme and enable you to pass the examination at the end of it, you will find that you can deal effectively with these problems.

Essential background information

Tutors can normally supply detailed information about examination requirements. Also, for a small fee, most examination boards will supply copies of past papers. These provide useful examples of the kinds of questions asked and they sometimes contain information about the weighting of questions in relation to marks.

It is this information, alongside your own written work, which is the basis for effective revision and so for examination success.

What examiners look for

Generally speaking, performance in examinations will also be improved if you are aware of the level of expected attainment. Advice from tutors is invaluable, but a careful consideration of the phrasing of examination questions can also be a great help. Questions for those studying for GCSE or equivalent levels usually include requests to 'describe' or 'give an account of' a particular topic. To answer such questions, the ability to grasp and remember sequences of information is needed. This must be presented in narrative form; it should also display an appropriate command of English.

Examinations at A Level or equivalent, up to and including degree level, make greater demands. Again tutors and past examination papers can provide vital pointers. At this level, candidates are commonly asked to 'discuss', to 'compare and contrast', to 'assess', to 'critically evaluate'. To meet these requirements, you need the ability to select and organize more complex bodies of knowledge. You should also be able to present it in the form of narrative and – where appropriate – analysis. Your use of English is also expected to be more sophisticated and your vocabulary more extensive, including the use of specialized terms, where necessary. Familiarity with a range of relevant critical opinion is also needed and you should be able to show an awareness of areas of academic debate and controversy.

Revision techniques

Revision is the process of looking over past work as a preparation for examination. It is an activity which can produce very good results – and reduce 'exam nerves' – if it is carefully planned and carried out in a systematic way. Black coffee and sleepless nights just before your exams rarely allow you to do justice to your talents!

Towards the end of a course, a review of your completed written work and of past examination papers will often indicate the existence of close links between examination questions and essays, assignments and project work. On this basis, you can select your own best work and use it for revision. Work which has been less successful should contain advice for improvement from a tutor and this can be followed up. For example, additional reading may be required to fill in gaps of understanding or errors of fact or interpretation. This can be done and recorded briefly in the form of notes, or in a fuller addition to the original piece of work.

When you have assembled, in this way, the body of your own work upon which you can reasonably expect the examination to focus, you are ready to begin the next stage of revision.

At this point, the selection and condensation of the key ideas and information contained in your work must be undertaken. The reason for this will be clear if you remember that *the time allowed to answer an examination question cannot be compared with the time needed to prepare an essay, assignment or project*. Again, even if it were possible to commit to memory every word you have ever written, it would not lead to success. This is because examinations are designed to probe your understanding of various aspects of a given subject and not simply to test the memory of the written work completed on a course.

What revision can do for you

- Extends your ability to assess your own knowledge and understanding.
- Provides an opportunity to analyse this in relation to the requirements of the examination board.
- Enables you to pass examinations and gain recognition for your talents.

Guidelines for successful revision

- Make sure you know well in advance when and where your exams will take place.
- Keep copies of all course documents, essay questions, titles of assignments, projects and reading lists on file.
- Make this the basis of your revision. Resist the temptation to try to start your course all over again from the beginning!
- Review your own assessed work, making a selection of that with the best grades.
- Compare your own work with the questions asked on past examination papers.
- At this stage, it is vital to make sure that you will have enough material to answer all the likely questions.
- If you decide to expand on what you have already got, look at less successful papers and see if you can improve them by careful editing, filling in gaps, correcting errors of fact or understanding.
- If you are really desperate for additional material, look back through your lecture notes or your class papers and build up from them bodies of knowledge relevant to examination questions.
- Reduce each piece of work to note form (see p. 124 above).

This is the material which you need to keep in mind for use in the examination room.

- Take time to practise answering examination questions.
- In the later stages of your revision, choose a question from a past paper and time yourself to answer it in one hour.
- Build this up because most exams require you to write for up to three hours at a stretch. This places great demands on your physical *and* mental stamina.

Taking examinations

Take it for granted that you will be nervous, no matter how well prepared you are! Adopt a positive mental attitude and think to yourself that trembling hands, shortness of breath, a rapidly beating heart and feelings of panic are signs that extra adrenalin is reaching the brain. Be assured that these reactions disappear quickly once you have started to write.

- Make sure you arrive on time.
- Remember to bring pens and a reliable watch.
- Take about five minutes to read all the questions and instructions on your paper.
- Select and mark the questions you are going to answer.
- Questions can be answered in any order as long as they are clearly numbered, so start off with something you feel confident about. (If you have revised well enough, you will start to relax at this point because you will recognize your chosen material.)
- All questions must be tackled, so allocate your time accordingly.
- Remember that results are calculated from an average of marks, so resist the temptation to spend all your time on your 'best' questions, ignoring all the rest.
- Time each question carefully. If it is not complete when allocated time is up, you *must* move on. Leave space to use later, if possible.
- Leave a few minutes at the end so that you can read quickly through what you have written.
- Correct errors, add extra items of information – even if in note form.
- Finally, remember that the last paper you sit is just as important as the first, so make sure you sustain your energy and your determination all the way through.

Conclusion

This chapter has emphasized the need to acquire the techniques necessary for successful study at a variety of levels and in a variety of contexts. Experience has shown that very many people who decide to resume their education or embark upon a training course are lacking not in ability, aptitude or intelligence – but simply in an understanding of appropriate study techniques.

Schools rarely provide instruction in them, yet other institutions often seem to assume that such skills are innate. This certainly is not the case. Study techniques have to be learned. They also need to be adapted and modified as experience is gained, courses progress and ambitions begin to develop further. The principles, practices and guidelines set out here are designed to lay sound foundations upon which personal, intellectual and academic progress can be built. We hope they will serve you well!

6

LOOKING TO THE FUTURE

Your future depends on the decisions you make as an individual and also, to a considerable extent, on the position of women in general, both in the work-force and in society as a whole. Therefore this chapter looks at the position of women as a developing sector of the employment market and their relationship to male workers. We include details of some organizations established to further women's position in the work-place and others which attempt to increase women's influence in society. The combination is essential. No doubt you have to be a successful politician every day, juggling your commitments and responsibilities. Equally, it is important to assess women's influence in government and government institutions, local councils, commercial organizations and other decision-making bodies. We need to consider how such influence might be increased. An increase would benefit all of us in the long run, both in terms of job prospects and in the importance given to child care needs and women's retraining.

You still have your own individual decisions and priorities, of course. So we have included case studies which indicate individual successes alongside the need for persistence and perseverance. You will notice also a need to reshape your outlook and aims from time to time.

It is clear that women with family responsibilities are now over a quarter of the labour force (see Figure 9) and this percentage is continuing to rise. This is very much a plus factor in favour of women who are obviously an *increasingly* large group of workers. Moreover, they comprise a group who are being encouraged more positively to continue working than at any time since the Second World War. There are two trends in operation here.

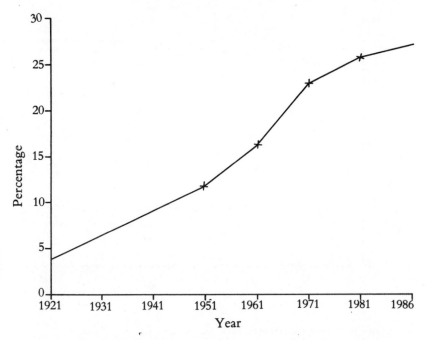

Figure 9 Married women as a percentage of the labour force (Source: *Department of Employment Gazette*)

Women seem more and more likely to have no break or only a short one from paid employment. Secondly, the reduction in the birth-rate has meant a smaller number of male workers entering the labour force. You may have noted that WRNS officers are actually going to sea, for the first time ever, since there are not enough male recruits to fill all the posts. Similar staff shortages elsewhere will give rise to wider opportunities for women. Female workers will become more visible and there will be greater pressures to promote some of them. So women should be able to insist on more flexible working hours and/or job-sharing in a much wider range of jobs.

Earnings

The 9 per cent increase in women's pay compared with men's between 1971 and 1981, rising from 63.7 per cent to 72.8 per cent (see Figure 10), was due to the implementation of the Equal

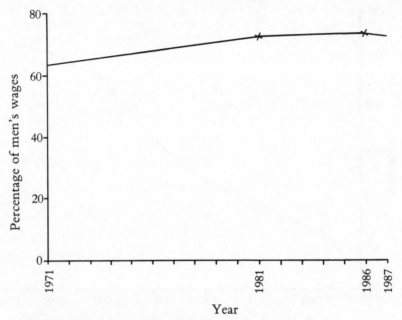

Figure 10 Women's earnings as a percentage of men's (Source: *Department of Employment Gazette*)

Opportunities and Sex Discrimination Acts. Since then the gap has hardly narrowed at all, women's pay hovering around the 74 per cent level in relation to men's. According to the TUC, women's average take-home pay is around 66 per cent of men's, since men have more opportunity for overtime and are given more bonus payments. Two factors help cause this imbalance. The discrepancy arises because women are still grouped mainly in a comparatively narrow range of occupations and still tend to be in the lower ranks, financially speaking, of most businesses and employing institutions.

There is undeniably a growing need for women workers but often the jobs on offer are still low-paid. Many of the jobs created in the 1980s were part-time and offered comparatively low salaries. This had the effect of helping along female recruitment but did not improve women's wages in general or their conditions of service. You may be one of the relatively few women who will be extremely successful. Inevitably, though, the majority of women will not get to the top. The wage structures which result in lower pay scales and lack of promotion in occupations dominated by women workers need to be significantly revised. It is unlikely to happen overnight. Such a revision does need the weight of social approval and implies again a need for an increase in women's participation in decision-making.

Individually you might consider working in an area where women are under-represented, for example, engineering. Such a career choice (or change) presents its own difficulties but wages are likely to be higher than for jobs in more female-dominated occupations. Keep in mind the optimist's message: you can often move on to a better-paid job once you have begun work. Look for such ladders from the beginning. If at all possible don't remain in a job you dislike which offers no likelihood of improvement. Move to a similar one where opportunities are more available for either more interesting or better-paid work – preferably both.

There are always regional variations in wages, as is obvious at the moment in the differences between wages in Scotland and the north of England compared with those in London and the South-east. Recessions come and go, changes in development may mean that some industries close down and others open elsewhere. Therefore in this book we have tended to look at the whole picture, the choices we have to make at different times of our lives, rather than considering just returning to work. Women have always had to be flexible and this is an excellent marketable quality in the present employment situation. However, some people who get jobs may find the job isn't there in two years or the business is moving elsewhere, and it is not feasible to uproot the family and follow the job. Equally you may find you have more time as children grow up or as your responsibilities for other dependants diminish. In that case you could take on a more demanding post or seek retraining. You must be prepared for alterations in your circumstances and consequently your goals will need to be reassessed. You should draw up a new 'ideal job specification' every year or so.

Age can still be a barrier. For example, most of the *new* jobs in 'Silicon Glen' in Scotland have turned out to be for relatively young women. One can only assume a financial reason for this, the assumption being that young men (and perhaps older women) would expect more money. Many employers have age limits in their minds, even if not in the job description. However, a number of agencies and sections of careers advisory services now deal specifically with older clients. And, if we follow the

American legislative example, there may be further laws to bring an end to discrimination in this area. It is likely that government agencies and market pressure will encourage firms to rethink their positions on early retirement and redundancy as the numbers of younger workers decrease.

Some women (and some employers) do not let age deter them. **Kathleen Jarman**, aged 52, is just undertaking her SEN (State Enrolled Nurse) qualifications, having started training as a nurse (SRN – State Registered Nurse) in 1956. She left full-time training when she had her first baby and was an auxiliary nurse for over twenty years, usually on night duty. She ran a cattery business for eight years and, now her husband has retired and her children have grown up, she has time to retrain once again. However, the SRN qualification has disappeared and the new RGN (Registered General Nurse) qualification would not take into account any of her previous training. Therefore she has decided to become an SEN.

> I'm enjoying it. I feel as if I'm completing something I started years ago. It would have been nice to have been an RGN but you have to think about the job prospects for a 56-year-old, which is what I'd be when I'd finished.

It is likely that another trend will continue and that is the decline in the number of lower-level jobs and an increase in jobs at a higher level. This is particularly marked at managerial and professional level but it is also affecting staff in secretarial and clerical jobs, in sales and marketing, in leisure and tourism and in craft work. You may consider it worthwhile not only updating your skills but also developing them further. You could then apply for a different range or category of work.

Job satisfaction and financial returns are often difficult to balance. Being a home help is an extremely useful, beneficial and often interesting occupation. Unfortunately at the present time the wages offered for these posts are not high. You may be able to weigh up the job interest and personal satisfaction versus the wages offered. Undoubtedly some better-paid jobs are more boring and less satisfying.

Case studies

Here we include five more case studies where women did not get where they wanted to immediately but they have continued to persevere.

Devi Sorefan:

I was a software programmer in Barclays Bank in 1970 but in 1974 took time off to have my third child. I joined a NOW course in 1978 and one of the topics was 'Setting up a Small Business'. As dressmaking was a hobby, I did a part-time City and Guilds 'Fashion Design and Dressmaking' course and subsequently sold a number of mouth-watering negligée sets but decided to return to professional work. Although I had the technical dressmaking skills, I lacked the business drive to charge realistic prices.

However, it was difficult to re-enter the job market because IT [information technology], the fastest growing industry, was going through a revolution. My previous computer knowledge needed updating dramatically. I chose to do a Master's degree as such a course would update my IT knowledge and give me a degree qualification which I did not have.

At first I could not get funding for my fees. Together with the Rights and Advice section of my Students' Union I wrote off to numerous charities. Eventually the fees were raised while I was on the course. Fortunately my youngest child was under 16 years and at school; we got Income Support so did not starve while I fed my brain IT knowledge. If he had been over 16 we would not have received Income Support.

My two sons experienced role reversals by doing the cooking while I studied and wrote my dissertation. (Tip – as long as there's plenty of food, never mind the cleaning.)

In retrospect, the full-time course has re-equipped me for the present job market. At the same time it helped me to get over becoming a single parent and to establish an identity apart from 'Mum' or 'single parent'.

It was difficult to find a full-time job at 40 plus. Frustratingly I was interviewed for a number of jobs since I fitted the gender, race equality and age discrimination slot – I could be interviewed as an applicant with an 'outside' chance. In January 1990 I was successful and joined a large organization as a trainer for a new software package. At 43 I feel I have eventually arrived and it's a good feeling.

Notes

1 For a list of charities, a book on charities in any library is useful.

2 See what category your personal circumstances fit, and write to relevant charities. There are specific charities for single parents (£50 is not to be sniffed at!).

3 There are sometimes local charities established long ago, who are willing to give to local residents for education purposes.

4 If you are a student in difficulties your Students' Union may suggest ways to help – where to get free stamps, how to manage debts, etc.

Iffat Ansari writes:

Like many other immigrants, when I came to Britain to join my husband, we had planned to stay for a few years and then go back. That is why I did not resign my job but came on unpaid leave. When my leave expired I did go back and stayed and worked there for a year. I returned again on unpaid leave. As our stay in Britain prolonged I sent my resignation to India. It was one of the most difficult decisions of my life.

For nearly eleven years I stayed at home and brought up our son. I do not remember being bored at home, but I did want to go back to work. Working with other people is stimulating and also means independence, and I missed both.

When I did go back to work, I didn't find it easy. Even though I had taught in two Indian universities, teaching in adult education was an entirely new experience. The all-pervasive structural and institutional racism in Britain is part of black people's life here. It undermines us at every level. We have to make adjustments to institutions which are white, mostly male and usually middle-class in spirit. They do not recognize our cultures, religions, languages or gender.

On the other hand it has been a positive experience from the point of view of my personal development. It has provided opportunities for some valuable in-service training. Working with Asian women has given me a very clear understanding of the dual oppression of race and gender that black women suffer. Above all it has given me the friendship and also solidarity with other women, mostly black but white too, which made returning to work a satisfying experience for me.

Georgina Bower fulfilled an ambition by further study but found it wasn't easy to change job direction:

I belong to a generation when it was considered, in some families, more important for the sons to receive higher education, rather than the daughters. I left school at 16, with seven O Levels, and went to work to help keep my younger brother at university.

After marriage, two children and a helpful NOW course I embarked on an Honours Degree Course in English at Sheffield City Polytechnic. Four years later I graduated with high hopes of obtaining a job *not* in the secretarial field – my original career. The reality came with facing the outside world again as a graduate nudging 50 years. The careers advice I was given was 'leave Sheffield' – totally impracticable as regards housing, husband's job and children's education.

I found secretarial work with a temporary employment agency and during the following nine months scoured job adverts in the local papers. I was rigorous in 'sifting' as I had neither time nor money to spare for those where I could not reasonably expect an interview. Several times I got no further than an initial telephone enquiry when I learnt I was out of touch, or over an age limit which seemed to stretch to only 35 years. In fact when a London-based firm moved to Sheffield and the bureau recruited on their behalf I was told that they only wanted staff 18–22 years of age. I was told that young members of staff didn't like working with old women or that older women couldn't mix with the younger generation. Having just left the Poly I knew this was not so and, anyway, who was this 'old' woman? I sent off twenty applications, some of which were acknowledged, and had five unsuccessful interviews.

I am now a personal secretary within the NHS. The main problem with secretarial work is the lack of promotion. The current practice of pigeon-holing people prevents cross-movement in that, for example, shorthand typists are necessary to service administrators. Administration seems to be largely in-service trained, taking about three years, which suggests that the return from a more mature person may not be high enough. I appreciate a degree is not a key to the future but I did hope it might widen my choice of employment. I do not, however, regret the time spent in study but I wish someone had made me aware of the 'real' state of employment for middle-aged mature students. In a catch-22 position I have reluctantly decided a job in the office is worth two in the adverts. On a personal level I feel fulfilled in having graduated, thus proving to myself I was just as capable as my brother.

Valerie Radford:

Since completing the NOW course in 1981 I have continued to carry the double disadvantage of being disabled and a married woman. The resettlement officer from the MSC decided my rightful place was to sit at a switchboard, which I managed to endure for six years, until leaving to care for elderly relatives. During this time I endeavoured to break free by applying for various jobs and courses. The reasons given for not accepting me for any of these included statements that I was too qualified to be considered disadvantaged despite being totally blind; I was not deprived because I already had a job; I was not sufficiently disabled to merit help on a special employment scheme; as a blind married woman

I would not find a job at my age, even if I completed the course; even with the City Council's policy of Equal Opportunities, I was never offered interviews for posts for which I was qualified.

I have just finished a year's work with an organization of disabled people. The busy round has now started again. I am back at the Jobclub, my c.v. is longer than ever and I am still wondering about setting myself up in business. Perhaps I could become an adviser to able-bodied, white, middle-aged men who are frustrated by being in work and having missed the joys of motherhood.

Jackie Smith:

I always wanted to be a painter and after A Levels took a pre-diploma art course. However, because of a lack of confidence and feeling alienated by a male-dominated, basic design-based course I failed to get on the course I really wanted. I started teacher training but realized at the end of the first year I definitely did not want to teach. After a year and a half during which I got married and changed jobs three times, including a stint in the Civil Service, I got on to an interior design course. I was persuaded by my husband, who was studying architecture, but I always had doubts about this particular course. Anyway after finishing I got a job as an interior designer and then I found myself pregnant after four months on the job. I was promised I could return part-time but because of a recession (which always hits the building trade first) I was no longer required.

I didn't fancy staying at home so I worked part-time for my father doing office work. I stuck that out for about three years and then became involved in co-counselling. Eventually I found work as a counsellor working for an abortion charity part-time. I had another child and continued at BPAS but lost some hours' work. After a few years I felt stuck, wanted to do something more creative and realized I would probably have to retrain. I heard about a one-year art therapy course. Amazingly I was accepted as they were very keen on mature students. The course was very intense and exhausting but my family were very supportive and I loved it. I realized at the age of 40 I had found something I really wanted to do and was good at.

Unfortunately there are not many jobs for art therapists as it is a relatively new profession and so I spent a year doing voluntary work, trying to get practical experience. Finally, last June I got a full-time job (this was always my objective, to be financially independent) as an art therapist. There is a slight problem in that I have to commute over eighty miles each day. After an eleven-hour day I still have a family to sort out but I love the work and just hope I have the energy to survive. It has been a long haul to get to this point. I have often felt a failure and that my working life has been extremely messy, but I have also felt I was capable of doing a lot more. I guess in the end you have to have faith in yourself and never give up.

Women at work

Troubles do not end once you have a job. Apart from your own domestic responsibilities, dependants, etc., and firms closing or reorganizing, you may not always see eye to eye with your employers. You may feel it is time you were promoted and you haven't been, that you need further training and courses are available if only you were given the time off work. Perhaps you have become pregnant and are unsure which benefits you can claim and whether you have a right to maternity leave and a job on your return. What happens if you are discriminated against, in terms of race or gender, are sexually harassed at work or become ill, particularly if that illness can be associated with the work you do? Suppose you are made redundant or are wrongfully dismissed, what can you claim and how should you act?

You can gain advice on questions of promotion, further training, health and safety at work and your statutory rights from a number of institutions and organizations. Their addresses are given at the end of the book. We look at a number of examples here.

Trade unions

It is misleading to assume that trade unions are only concerned with pay and, towards that end, organizing strikes. One of their main functions is to deal with conditions of service in the workplace, and pay of course will come under discussion. A union will give you advice on training, health and safety at work, your statutory rights including maternity and paternity leave, and pensions (even if your job is not covered by an occupational pension scheme). Unions can be very helpful nowadays for part-time workers, whose rights for many years were as neglected by trade unions as by employers. Five times as many women as men are part-time workers, and this may account for trade union indifference in the past. Part-time earnings per hour are lower than the average hourly earnings of full-time workers. However, since women will be encouraged back into work during the 1990s on a part-time as well as a full-time basis, these conditions may well improve. If you join a trade union you can find out what is happening not only in your particular work area but in similar employment elsewhere. You will be given advice and practical help on negotiation and entitlement. If you are not sure which union to join, write to the TUC, which will send you the relevant information.

By the end of 1989 women accounted for over a third of union membership and the proportion is increasing. The TUC has a women's section which has produced a charter for women at work and a resource pack on child care. The trade union movement is now well aware of the importance of including women at all levels of its decision-making, although like most other organizations the higher you go the fewer women you tend to find. Nevertheless they are making strenuous efforts to include more women in business meetings by providing child-care facilities and are also taking up what might be termed 'women's issues' on their agenda. Many of these issues concern workers of both sexes, for example child care, good practice in staff development and training. When the issue is one of discrimination or sexual harassment unions often work with other organizations to defend your rights. Directives from the European Economic Community may well prove helpful to women, since many of the EEC countries have much better records as regards maternity benefits and employment rights for women than Britain does. Unions will be able to advise you about such developments.

The Equal Opportunities Commission

The EOC aims to create equal opportunities for both women and men, particularly as regards work, education, consumer rights and welfare benefits. They will give you free advice on any of these areas, if you consider you have a grievance, and explain how you could take your case to an industrial tribunal or a lawcourt. There still appears to be in-built discrimination against women in employment, as Elspeth Howe has pointed out in her recent survey, *Women at the Top* (the report of the Hansard Society Commission, 1990). Sometimes in specific cases the EOC helps an individual take up a case and even pays legal costs, particularly if the case is an important one for other workers. They have published a large number of leaflets and good practice guides and regularly comment on existing laws and government policies. They work with trade unions and employers to encourage women to enter employment traditionally taken up by men.

Do get in touch with the Commission very quickly if you consider you have been discriminated against because you are a woman, or if discrimination is taking place in your work-place generally against women, or in the schools which your children attend, or has occurred in any of the financial transactions you

have engaged in recently. There are difficulties in proving discrimination and the rate of successful cases is not high. However,
a study of women who had taken their cases to court or tribunal
found that women were glad they had fought their battle even
when discrimination was not proven.

The Industrial Society – Pepperell Unit

There are a number of organizations seeking to promote equal
opportunities within society, since such a policy is clearly more
efficient in the long run. The Industrial Society is concerned to
utilize to the full talents within the entire work-force, and to
encourage those seeking work to develop their potential. Within
the Society the Pepperell Unit is concerned with greater equality
of opportunity in employment, including minority ethnic groups.
It works with organizations and employers, runs conferences on
specific issues such as in-house tráining but also on wider topics
such as child care, career breaks, dual careers and relocation. It
caters for employers, careers advisers and sixth-formers and other
students. Many of the course fees are quite high unless you are
in work and can persuade your firm to send you along for retraining, development of managerial or personal effectiveness skills,
or to attend a course on 'Making Equal Opportunities Happen',
and thus help in the potential development of your organization
as a whole. If you can persuade your firm to do so, then you
are well away. However, if you do not, it is useful to keep the
work of the Pepperell Unit in mind, and use it as a bench-
mark. You can try to persuade your own employers to run staff
development courses on a similar model, or enquire if your local
education provider (a Local Authority, polytechnic, university,
further education or tertiary college) runs such courses.

Occupational associations

There are a number of associations geared to particular occupations, for example the Women's Engineering Society, Women
in Publishing, Women in Management, Women and Manual
Trades. Some have been established for decades but more of them
appear each year, so keep looking in the files at information
centres. These associations will give advice to women thinking
of entering or rejoining work in their professional area, and will

also give advice on matters relating to generally accepted working conditions in that occupation. They are usually very supportive and promotional, wishing to encourage more women to enter their work field and aim for higher positions once they are there.

Social change

There might be considerable social change if more women were encouraged to enter public life as MPs or councillors. At present only 6.3 per cent of British MPs are female and the percentage doesn't appear to be likely to change very much. There might be changes if Britain were to gain a more equitable voting system which would be friendlier to women. For example, in West Germany the electoral system includes both constituency members and a top-up of extra MPs to make the proportions tally with the votes cast. Women tend to do much better under such a system where access to public life can be monitored in terms of representation (see Figure 11).

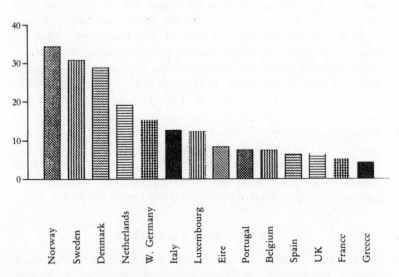

Figure 11 Percentage of female representatives in European Parliaments

The 300 Group

The name indicates one of the Group's major aims: to have 300 women MPs in Parliament. It also has much wider objectives. The Group encourages women of all political parties and those who do not belong to such a party to take an active part in the country's decision-making. It wishes to create a climate of opinion which regards as natural the participation of women in public life. It organizes workshops where women can learn skills and gain the training needed to make them effective candidates for Councils, Parliament or the European Parliament. There are many local groups who organize local meetings and workshops on assertion training and public speaking as well as information sessions on public bodies. The 300 Group claims that the all-party aspect works (perhaps another example of women's co-operation?) and this might make the association extremely helpful to you.

With confidence and experience maybe you would make an excellent campaigner, councillor or MP. With more women in such positions the status accorded to jobs such as home helps might change radically. It is already known that male and female voters have very different opinions about child benefits, but of course the legislators are predominantly male. More women in public life might change the level of importance granted to many issues.

As a beginning, you can write to your MP (male or female) to indicate the way you feel laws should change or benefits be altered. Letters do appear to make some difference to MPs' conclusions, even if they are only concerned about voting patterns in their constituencies. And, after all, writing letters is often good practice for getting into the habit of writing or for continuing it once you have begun. Why not start now?

POSTSCRIPT

Tinker tailor soldier sailor
Rich woman home help comedian cook

(continue as long as you like, until you find the job you feel is
most appropriate)

If it has taken you one week or six months to work through this
book you are now in a position to reassess your goals and see
how far your planning has developed. Select the items which
might be most useful to you and concentrate on them. Remember, self-development is a continuing process. You can't expect
to make one great leap forward and then sit back. The leap in
itself will have changed your situation and set up repercussions.
Some parts of the book should, we hope, be useful to you for a
long time. And, although it is written particularly for women,
the study notes and interview sections can be very helpful (as we
have discovered) to teenagers of both sexes. We have often
thought that the best career advice for young girls of 13 and 14
would come from women aged 25 to 40. It's a pity such advice
sessions are not established formally in schools.

The very best of luck for the whole of the rest of your work
and life, paid and unpaid!

Moira, Gill and Gina

READING LIST

WOMEN AND SKILLS FOR SUCCESS

Chapman, Jane *Women Working it Out* (COIC, 1987)
Cooke, Ivana *Women Mean Business* (Everywoman, 1990)
Davidson, Marilyn *Reach for the Top: A Woman's Guide to Success in Business and Management* (Piatkus, 1985)
Dickson, Anne *A Woman In Your Own Right* (Quartet, 1982)
Slipman, Sue *Helping Ourselves to Power: A Handbook for Women on the Skills of Public Life* (Pergamon, 1986)

WOMEN AND WORK

Hodgkinson, Liz *Working Woman's Guide* (Thorsons, 1985)
LaRouche, Janice *Strategies for Women at Work* (Unwin, 1984)
Moulder, Cathy and Sheldon, Pat *Back to Work: A Practical Guide for Women* (Kogan Page, regularly updated)
Velmans, Marianne and Litvinoff, Sarah *Working Mother: A Practical Handbook* (Corgi, 1987)

WOMEN AND LANGUAGE

Coates, Jennifer *Women, Men and Language* (Longman, 1986)
Graddol, David and Swann, Joan *Gender Voices* (Basil Blackwell, 1989)
Swift, K. and Miller, C. *Words and Women* (Gollancz, 1977)
Spender, Dale *Man Made Language* (Routledge and Kegan Paul, 1980)

WOMEN AND STRESS

Cooper, Cary *Living with Stress* (Penguin, 1988)
Cooper, Cary and Davidson, Marilyn *High Pressure – Working Lives of Women Managers* (Fontana, 1982)
Ernst, Sheila and Goodison, Lucy *In Our Own Hands: A Book of Self-help Therapy* (Women's Press, 1981)
Kirsta, Alix *Book of Stress Survival: How to Relax and De-Stress Your Life* (Unwin, 1986)

WOMEN AND STUDY

Beddowes, Christopher *Returning to Study* (Heinemann Educational, 1989)

Buzan, Tony *Use Your Head* (BBC, 1989)

Gilbert, John K. *Staying the Course: How to Survive in Higher Education* (Kogan Page, 1989)

Heap, Brian *How to Choose Your Degree Course* (Trotman, 1989)

Marshall, Lorraine and Rowland, Frances *A Guide to Learning Independently* (Open University, 1989)

Newby, Michael *Writing: A Guide for Students* (Cambridge University Press, 1989)

Percy, Diane *Adult Study Tactics* (Macmillan, 1989)

Taylor, Felicity *After School: A Guide to Post School Opportunities* (Kogan Page, 1989)

Rosier, Iris and Earnshaw, Lyn *Mature Students' Handbook* (Trotman, 1989)

USEFUL ADDRESSES

Careers Office: Look in your telephone directory or ask at your local library for the address of your local office

Careers for Women, Women's Career Counselling, 2 Valentine Place, London, SE1 8QH, tel. 071 401 2280

Citizens Advice Bureau: look in your telephone directory or ask at your local library for the address of the local CAB office

Commission for Racial Equality (CRE), Elliot House, 10–12 Allington Street, London SW1E 5EH, tel. 071 828 7022

Co-operative Development Agency, Broadmead House, 21 Panton Street, London SW1Y 4DR, tel. 071 839 2988, and Holyoak House, Hanover Street, Manchester M60 0AS, tel. 061 833 9379

Equal Opportunities Commission (EOC), Overseas House, Quay Street, Manchester M3 3HN, tel. 061 833 9244

Industrial Common Ownership Movement, 8 Sussex Street, London SW1, tel. 071 828 2321

Jobcentre: look in your telephone directory or ask at your local library for the address of your local office

National Advisory Centre on Careers for Women, 8th Floor, Artillery House, Artillery Row, London SW1P 1RT, tel. 071 799 2129

New Ways to Work, 309 Upper Street, London N1 2TY, tel. 071 226 4026

Open University, Walton Hall, Milton Keynes, MK7 6AA, tel. 0908 274066

Pepperell Unit, The Industrial Society, Robert Hyde House, 48 Bryanston Square, London W1H 7LN, tel. 071 262 2401

300 Group (National Office), 36–37 Charterhouse Square, London EC1M 6EA, tel. 071 600 2390

Trades Union Congress, Congress House, Great Russell Street, London WC1B 3LS, tel. 071 636 4030

Women and Manual Trades, 52–54 Featherston Street, London EC1Y 8RT, tel. 071 251 9192

Women and Training, Hewmar House, 120 London Road, Gloucester GL1 3PL, tel. 0452 309330

Women in Business, Small Business Bureau, Suite 46, Westminster

Palace Gardens, Artillery Row, London SW1P 1RR, tel. 071 976 7262/3

Women in Management, 64 Marryat Road, Wimbledon, London SW19 5BN, tel. 081 944 6332

Women in Publishing, c/o J. Whitaker and Sons, 12 Dyott Street, London WC1A 1DF, tel. 071 836 8911

Women Returners' Network, c/o Ruth Michaels, Hatfield Polytechnic, College Lane, Hatfield, Hertfordshire AL10 9AB

Women's Engineering Society, Department of Civil Engineering, Imperial College, London SW7 7BU, tel. 071 589 5111 ext. 4731

Workers' Educational Association, 9 Upper Berkeley Street, London W1H 8BY, tel. 071 402 5608; the London Office can give you the address of local contacts

Working Mothers' Association, 77 Holloway Road, London N7 8J2, tel. 071 700 5771

INDEX

physical recreation 36
Playgroups' Association 42

self-assessment 10
self-development 22, 24
self-employment 90
Sex Discrimination Act 148
sexual harassment 96–7
speculative job applications 74–6
Spender, Dale 55, 163
stress 43–4

Thatcher, Margaret 54
Trade Unions 148, 157–8, 165

Women and Manual Trades 96,
  159, 165
Women in Business 96, 165
Women in Management 159, 166
Women in Publishing 159, 166
Women's Engineering Society 42,
  159, 166
Women's Institute 42
work options: flexible working 89;
  job sharing 87–8; part-time
  work 87; running a business
  90–4; working from home 86
writing 55–66; of essays 133–40;
  and therapy 65